On the occasion of the observance
of the 400th anniversary of Michelangelo's death
and in celebration
of the Vatican Pavilion of the Holy See
at the New York World's Fair

· 1964 ·

MICHELANGELO:
THE PIETA
AND OTHER MASTERPIECES

JOSEF VINCENT LOMBARDO

LITT.D., PH.D., LL.D.

Queens College, The City University of New York

A POCKET BOOK SPECIAL

Published by Pocket Books, Inc.

New York, 1965

NIHIL OBSTAT:
    Thomas W. Smiddy, S.T.L.
    Censor Librorum

IMPRIMATUR:
    ✠ Bryan Josephus McEntegart, D.D., LL.D.
    Episcopus Bruklyniensis

BRUKLYNI
    Die xxiv februarii, 1964

TO

HIS EMINENCE

FRANCIS CARDINAL SPELLMAN

ARCHBISHOP OF NEW YORK

AND

HIS EXCELLENCY

THE MOST REVEREND BRYAN J. McENTEGART

BISHOP OF BROOKLYN

CONTENTS

LIST OF ILLUSTRATIONS 8   INTRODUCTION 9

PART ONE

Pietà *a fusion of Christian faith and Neoplatonism / Michelangelo's family and early childhood / Early interest in drawing and painting / Friendship with Francesco Granacci / A pupil of Bertoldo di Giovanni / Invited to live in the palace of Lorenzo de' Medici /* Madonna of the Stairs / Battle of the Centaurs / *Flight to Bologna and commission for San Domenico / Sojourn in Bologna / Return to Florence in 1495 /* Youthful St. John the Baptist / *Stylistic characteristics and sculptural motifs /* Bacchus.

11

PART TWO

Pietà *restates medieval doctrine of Divine Purpose / Michelangelo commissioned to carve* Pietà / *Contract for* Pietà / *Origins of the theme / Antecedents of Michelangelo's* Pietà / *No parallel to* Pietà / *Aesthetic considerations / Christ not portrayed as a cadaver / Christ and Madonna a sculptural entity / Size of Madonna of the* Pietà / *Design of the* Pietà / *Madonna's youthfulness explained / Influence of Neoplatonism on Michelangelo / Savonarola's influence on Michelangelo / Mary in the* Bruges Madonna.

27

PART THREE

Pope John XXIII consents to exhibit Pietà *at World's Fair / Impact of* Pietà *on American taste and culture / Removal of* Pietà *from St. Peter's protested / Edward Kinney's role in transportation of* Pietà / *Cardinal Spellman and the Elgin Marbles / Precautions taken to transport* Pietà *safely / Official unveiling of* Pietà *in New York, April 19, 1964.*

49

NOTES 55   SELECTED BIBLIOGRAPHY 59   INDEX 61   BIOGRAPHICAL NOTES 64

ILLUSTRATIONS

1. Pietà (color). *View of statue without pedestal.*

2. Pietà (color). *Detail of Madonna's head.*

3. Pietà (color). *Detail of Christ's head.*

4. Pietà (color). *View from above showing the full figure of Christ.*

5. Pietà (color). PHOTO: *C. Harrison Conroy, New York.*

6. La Cappella della Pietà, *St. Peter's Basilica, Rome.*

7. Pietà. *As it appears above eye level.*

8. Pietà. *Detail of the right side.*

9. Battle of the Centaurs, *Casa Buonarroti, Florence.*

10. Madonna of the Stairs, *Casa Buonarroti, Florence.*

11. Youthful St. John the Baptist, *Piero Tozzi Collection, New York.*

12. Youthful St. John the Baptist, *Piero Tozzi Collection, New York.*

13. Youthful St. John the Baptist, *Piero Tozzi Collection, New York.*

14. Bacchus, *Museo Nazionale, Florence.*

15. Pietà. *View of right side.*

16. Pietà. *Detail of Christ's head.*

17. Pietà. *Detail of Christ's body.*

18. Pietà. *View of left side.*

19. Pietà. *Detail of Madonna's head.*

20. Pietà. *Detail of Christ's right hand.*

21. Pietà. *Detail of Christ's right foot.*

22. Pietà. *Detail of Madonna's left hand.*

23. Pietà. *Detail of Christ's left hand.*

24. Pietà. *As it appears at eye level in St. Peter's Basilica.*

25. Giuliano de' Medici, *Medici Chapel, Church of San Lorenzo, Florence.*

26. Lorenzo de' Medici, *Medici Chapel, Church of San Lorenzo, Florence.*

27. Bruges Madonna. *Detail of Christ Child.*

28. Pietà. *Detail of Madonna's face.*

29. Bruges Madonna. *Detail of Madonna's face.*

30. Pietà. *Detail showing Michelangelo's name inscribed on* cintura *or band.*

31. Bruges Madonna, *Church of Notre-Dame, Bruges.*

32. Moses, *Church of San Pietro in Vincoli, Rome.*

33. Pietà. *Statue showing the two bronze angels and halo before their removal in 1927.*

34. Pietà. *Cathedral of Florence.*

35. Pietà. *Detail of Christ's body.*

INTRODUCTION

THE FACTS of Michelangelo's life were derived in the main from original sources: Giorgio Vasari's (1511-1574) *Le vite de' più eccellenti architetti, pittori et scultori italiani*, published in Florence in 1550 and followed by a second enlarged edition in 1568; and Ascanio Condivi's (1525-1574) *Vita di Michelangelo Buonarroti*, which appeared in Rome in 1553. The edition of Vasari's *Vite* used was that of Gaetano Milanesi, published in Florence in 1878-1885; and Condivi's, the second edition of 1746, printed in Florence. Vasari and Condivi were friends and contemporaries of Michelangelo. Charles de Tolnay's authoritative studies on Michelangelo were also consulted, as were the writings of other scholars, Italian and German. All translations from the Italian were made by the author.

For the comparative analyses and aesthetic critique of the *Pietà*, the author relied upon his own research and observations during his studies in Rome and at the University of Florence. Some of the critical evaluations in this text do not appear anywhere in the vast literature on Michelangelo.

The author wishes to express his gratitude to His Eminence, Cardinal Amleto Giovanni Cicognani, *Segretario di Stato di Sua Santità*, for his gracious assistance and for the beautiful photographs used in this study; to the Vatican scholar, Dr. Deoclecio Redig de Campos of *Monumenti, Musei e Gallerie Pontificia, Stato della Città Vaticano;* and to *Fotografia Pontificia Francesco Giordani* of Rome. Deep appreciation for assistance and encouragement is also extended to the Right Reverend Monsignor Terence J. Cooke, Chancellor of the Archdiocese of New York; to the Right Reverend Monsignor Timothy J. Flynn, Director of Information of the Archdiocese of New York; to Dr. Vincent James Fontana, Dr. Hannibal DeBellis, Dr. Antonio Rottino, Dr. Milton Helpern, Dr. Wallace W. McCrory, Dr. Louis L. Bergmann, Dr. Henry R. Shinefield, and Henry A. LaFarge, senior editor of *Art News*.

Special thanks are due to the sponsoring commission of American prelates which made possible the Vatican Pavilion and its notable exhibits at the New York World's Fair. The commission comprises the following church dignitaries: His Eminence, Francis Cardinal Spellman, Archbishop of New York, President; His Excellency, The Most Reverend Bryan J. McEntegart, Bishop of Brooklyn, Vice President; His Eminence James

Francis Cardinal McIntyre, Archbishop of Los Angeles; His Eminence, Richard Cardinal Cushing, Archbishop of Boston; His Eminence, Albert Cardinal Meyer, Archbishop of Chicago; His Eminence, Joseph Cardinal Ritter, Archbishop of St. Louis; His Eminence, Lawrence Cardinal Shehan, Archbishop of Baltimore (MD.); the Most Reverend Thomas A. Boland, Archbishop of Newark (N.J.); the Most Reverend Patrick A. O'Boyle, Archbishop of Washington (D.C.); the Most Reverend John J. Krol, Archbishop of Philadelphia (PA.); the Most Reverend Walter P. Kellenberg, Bishop of Rockville Centre (N.Y.); the Most Reverend John W. Comber, M.M., Maryknoll (N.Y.); and the Most Reverend Edward E. Swanstrom, National Catholic Welfare Conference.

The Vatican Pavilion Committee consists of the Right Reverend Monsignor Terence J. Cooke, Chairman; the Right Reverend Monsignor James W. Asip; the Right Reverend Monsignor Francis M. Costello; the Right Reverend Monsignor Timothy J. Flynn; the Right Reverend Monsignor John J. Gorman; the Right Reverend Monsignor Raymond S. Leonard; the Reverend Joseph T. Lahey and Mr. Edward M. Kinney.

J. V. L.

October, 1964

· PART ONE ·

Pietà a fusion of Christian faith and Neoplatonism / Michelangelo's family and early childhood / Early interest in drawing and painting / Friendship with Francesco Granacci / A pupil of Bertoldo di Giovanni / Invited to live in the palace of Lorenzo de' Medici / Madonna of the Stairs / Battle of the Centaurs / Flight to Bologna and commission for San Domenico / Sojourn in Bologna / Return to Florence in 1495 / Youthful St. John the Baptist / Stylistic characteristics and sculptural motifs / Bacchus

CHRISTIAN FAITH and a new promise of hope for all humanity are revelations vividly and beautifully expressed in Michelangelo's *Pietà* (1498-1500) in St. Peter's Basilica in Rome (*pl. 5, 6*). In this elegant and spiritually stirring group, Michelangelo combines Christian doctrine with the Neoplatonic ideal of beauty.

Also known as the *Madonna della Febbre*, *Pietà* is the name given to the theme portraying the dead body of Christ lying in the arms of His grieving Mother. *Pietà* is an Italian word derived from the Latin *pietas*, the root for the English words pity and piety. It also means sorrow, grief, compassion.

Michelangelo's *Pietà* is placed high above the altar of the Cappella della Pietà, the first chapel in the right aisle as one enters St. Peter's Basilica. It is placed too high above eye level to be seen advantageously (*pl. 7*). In 1962, after the first session of the Ecumenical Council in Rome summoned by Pope John XXIII (1959-1963), the *Pietà* was lowered 4'9" and tilted 5.9" towards the spectator to correct this difficulty, but the visual problem was not wholly solved.[1]

A white Cross is set in the multicolored marble wall of the chapel behind the statue of the *Pietà*. The proportions of the Cross in relation to the two figures of Christ and Mary leave much to be desired. Mary sits on a roughly hewn rock, and the marble Cross is intended to simulate the tragedy at Golgotha, a rocky hillock in Jerusalem about fifteen feet higher than the surrounding terrain where Christ was crucified.[2]

The *Pietà* itself rests on an oval pedestal of red marble crowned by a white cornice or molding (*pl. 5*). The whole setting for the *Pietà* is too pictorial for a marble statue, 68.5" high, 76.7" wide, and 25.1" deep.[3]

Michelangelo Buonarroti (1475-1564) was born in Tuscany and achieved great fame as a sculptor, painter, architect and poet. His activity was boundless. He was a humanist in his search for ideal beauty and he elevated art to a dignity and influence unknown before his time. A good Christian, he absorbed all the knowledge and attributes of the fifteenth century Italian Renaissance and culminated the High Renaissance in Italy in the early part of the sixteenth century. Mannerism and Baroque, which followed the High Renaissance in Italy, stem directly from the creative genius of his work in sculpture, painting and architecture.

According to tradition, Michelangelo's family descended from the Counts of Canossa. His family name was Simoni, later changed to Buonarroti when his father settled in Florence. His father, Ludovico di Lionardo Buonarroti Simoni, married Francesca, daughter of Neri di Miniato del Sera. On March 6, 1475, Ludovico recorded in his diary the birth of Michelangelo at Caprese, a rustic hamlet near Arezzo and south of Florence. Tucked away in the mountains of that region, the small but beautiful village was situated on the watershed between the Tiber and Arno Rivers. Caprese had been under Florentine rule since 1389.[4] Michelangelo was the second of five sons.

Soon after his birth, the Buonarroti family left Caprese, where Ludovico had been *Podestà*, or Mayor, and returned to Florence. The infant Michelangelo was brought to Settignano, about three miles from Florence, to be nursed by the daughter of a stonecarver. She, too, was married to a stonecutter.[5] His mother was too frail and delicate in health to nurse her own child. In later years, Michelangelo used to joke about it by saying that he took to the sculptor's chisel and hammer naturally, attributing his proclivity to the fact that he had been nursed by the milk of a stonecarver's daughter.

Ludovico sent his young son to Maestro Francesco da Urbino who conducted a school in Florence for instruction in grammar and writing. But the young boy's interests were elsewhere. Rather than learn the fundamentals of Italian and possibly Latin grammar, he preferred to draw and sketch. Rhetoric had little appeal for him, but he did spend many delightful hours in the Brancacci Chapel in the Church of the

Carmine in Florence, sketching from the great fresco paintings of Masaccio (1401-1428).[7]

Michelangelo's irresistible yearning to draw manifested itself at an extremely early age and this interest made him spend most of his leisure time with youngsters of his own age who were apprentices in the studios of various Florentine painters and sculptors. Francesco Granacci, an intimate friend six years his senior, was a pupil in the studio of Domenico Ghirlandaio (1449-1494), and encouraged the embryonic sculptor to draw and paint.[8] Domenico maintained a *bottega*, assisted by his two brothers, Davide (1452-1525) and Benedetto (1458-1497). Ridolfo (1483-1561), Domenico's son, was also an apprentice at this time. Domenico was one of the foremost painters of his day.[9]

In 1488, when Michelangelo was a youth of thirteen, his father apprenticed him to Domenico for a period of three years, beginning on the first of April.[10] However, one day young Michelangelo and his friend Granacci went to see the collection of classical sculpture in the Medici gardens on Piazza di San Marco in Florence. Michelangelo was so overwhelmed by their beauty that he no longer returned to Domenico's studio, preferring to draw from the ancient statues.[11]

Vasari's report of Michelangelo's departure from Domenico is somewhat different. He relates that Lorenzo the Magnificent (1449-1492) appointed Bertoldo di Giovanni (c. 1420-1491), a pupil of the famous fifteenth century sculptor, Donatello (c. 1386-1466), to oversee his collection and to assist young men seeking instruction. Lorenzo had established an art school in Florence under his patronage in 1489 to encourage the study of art. Lorenzo asked Domenico and other masters to send their most promising apprentices to his free academy. Domenico is believed to have dispatched Granacci and Michelangelo. Bertoldo, supervisory head of the art academy, thus became Michelangelo's master.[12]

One day Michelangelo was working on a marble mask of a faun he was copying when Lorenzo chanced by in his customary stroll through the gardens and stopped to watch the young sculptor. He was so deeply impressed by the youngster's skill and the beauty of the mask, that he asked to talk to Michelangelo's father.[13]

Lorenzo, who saw great promise in the young man, asked Ludovico for consent to have his teenage son live under his guardianship. Michelangelo was given a room in Lorenzo's palace and five ducats a month. His status in Lorenzo's household was that of an adopted son and honored guest.[14]

Vasari writes that from 1490 to the death of Lorenzo on April 8, 1492, Michelangelo lived in the Palazzo de' Medici and dined with Lorenzo's children and distinguished guests.[15]

According to Vasari, Michelangelo left Domenico's studio in 1489. Condivi is mistaken when he says that Michelangelo lived with Lorenzo for about two years prior to his death. Actually he stayed with Lorenzo *Il Magnifico* for three significant years, spanning the spring of 1489 and the spring of 1492.[16] Significant because Lorenzo's palace was the meeting place of the most illustrious men of his time—men of letters, poets, philosophers, musicians, artists—and the leading Neoplatonists: Marsilio Ficino (1433-1499), Lorenzo's tutor, a theologian, philosopher and author of *Theologia platonica;* Giovanni Pico della Mirandola (1463-1494), called Pico, humanist and scholar; Cristoforo Landino (1424-1492), scholar and author of *Disputationes camaldulenses,* whose ideas were a source of inspiration to Michelangelo; Girolamo Benivieni (1453-1542), poet and author of the Neoplatonic *De lo amore celeste.* Ficino and Pico established the Platonic Academy in Florence under the patronage of its founder, Cosimo de' Medici (1389-1464), and continued by his son.

Two poets of the Platonic Academy who achieved widespread fame were Lorenzo himself and Angelo Poliziano (1454-1494), humanist and tutor of Lorenzo's children (Piero, Giovanni, later Pope Leo x; Giuliano, Duc de Nemours; Lucrezia, Maddalena, Contessina), who lived in the same palace and encouraged Michelangelo in his work. The young sculptor spent his time among these learned men, listening to their discourses and polemics, their poetry and philosophic theories.[17] His formative years were spent in this contagious and stimulating environment of great men. Their erudition fired Michelangelo's thoughts and creative imagination. They exposed him to abstract logic and thought in their debates on universal and absolute truth. Michelangelo, young, impressionable and eager, gave searching thought to the ideas expounded by these scholars who formed the cultural family of Lorenzo the Magnificent and the cultural heritage of Michelangelo.

That the glorification of beauty was a manifestation of the divine; that the morality and dignity of man were an inheritance from God to enable man to ennoble his life on earth; that Christianity and Neoplatonism were compatible and valid means of expressing universal truth; that man harbored within himself the means for his own salvation through his own deeds and inner goodness—out of these fertile seeds of thought and inspiration emerged Michelangelo's spiritual aspiration and aesthetic convictions.

Many of the thoughts and ideas Michelangelo absorbed from this circle of literary men and scholars are expressed in two marble bas-reliefs, both in the Casa Buonarroti in Florence, executed during his stay with Lorenzo between 1490 and 1492: the *Madonna of the Stairs* (*pl. 10*), a religious subject, and the *Battle of the Centaurs* (*pl. 9*), a pagan theme believed by Vasari and Condivi to have been inspired by Poliziano. Both bas-reliefs are mentioned by Vasari in his 1568 edition of *Le vite* and by Condivi.[18]

The *Madonna of the Stairs* (21.8″ high, 15.7″ wide) is stylistically significant in that it anticipates the *contrappósto* and other design motifs of Michelangelo's later work. Sitting on a large block of marble at the foot of a flight of steps, the Virgin fills the greater part of the rectangular composition, an arrangement suggested by the stelae or sepulchral reliefs of ancient Greece. The Virgin's Grecian head is in profile and her body is shown with a slight turn toward the spectator. An onyx cameo in the Medici Collection depicting the *Judgment of Paris* may have served as Michelangelo's model for the seated Virgin. Juno, in this cameo, is seated on a block of stone and resembles the seated position of the Virgin. It is a known fact that during the time he lived at his palace, young Michelangelo spent many hours studying and admiring Lorenzo's gem collection.[19]

A bas-relief of *Santa Cecilia* attributed both to Donatello (1386-1466) and his pupil, Desiderio da Settignano (c. 1430-1464), probably suggested the sculptural design of the Virgin's head. *Santa Cecilia*, however is carved with more delicacy and refinement—it does not have the prominent brow of Michelangelo's Virgin. Neither does it show the undercutting used by Donatello or Desiderio to create a more vivid illusion of form and space. Both reliefs are flat, or *schiacciáto,* as the Italians call it. A loose, free-flowing mantle envelops the Virgin's body; it covers her head which is set against a halo like a cameo.

The robust Christ Child is shown with His back to the audience, writhing, suckling or sleeping quietly in His mother's arms. Silhouetted against His mother, with whom He is inseparable as one substantive being, the Christ Child seems to spring forth from her body.

Linear perspective, which deals with line and size, is the pictorial means of creating the illusion of space and depth on a flat surface. In the *Madonna of the Stairs,* depth is defined by diminishing the size of the figures—the Virgin is the largest figure and she projects further from the background than the middle figure which, in turn, is raised higher than the two children in the upper distance. By varying the size and projection of his figures, Michelangelo created a series of recessive planes, all parallel to the picture plane and parallel to each other, to establish the fact that one figure is further back in space than the preceding one. This device is the stock-in-trade of the painter, and it is applied to the bas-relief—which has the same two-dimensional point of view as a painting—when the sculptor attempts and desires a pictorial effect, as in Lorenzo Ghiberti's so-called *Gates of Paradise*, the principal bronze doors of the Baptistry of San Giovanni of the Cathedral of Florence.

In nature, the human eye sees distant objects with less clarity. In the *Madonna of the Stairs*, the foreground figure of the Virgin is more detailed than the middle-ground figure leaning over the wall balustrade; this figure is more detailed than the two roughed-out figures on the top landing of the stairs. Consequently, Michelangelo created space and depth, not only by line and size, but also by observing the visual phenomenon that sees foreground objects with greater detail and clarity than distant ones.

The figure in the middle-ground, stretched over the wall flanking the steps, helps to define the space between the seated Virgin and the two little figures clustered together. This figure also serves as a transition, together with the diagonal of the wall, between the frontal and back planes of the composition. The view of the wall shown is the thickness of the top and corresponds to the balustrade of a staircase. Its sides are not shown. All exterior staircases in Italy are flanked by a solid wall. As a diagonal element of design, it brings together in a unified system the Virgin in the frontal plane with the two roughly hewn figures in the upper left-hand corner. The steep but short diagonal to the immediate right of the two little figures is the edge of the horizontal wall of the top landing. Both children provide needed balance for the figure of the Virgin. The setting of the *Madonna of the Stairs* is conceived above eye level. Only the risers of the steps are visible, for example, and they diminish in height as they ascend to the top—the treads, or the tops of the steps, are not represented. A border, cut from the original slab of marble, enframes the bas-relief.

Many elements in this composition recur in Michelangelo's later sculptures. A clear affinity exists, for example, between the position of the Virgin's two hands and those in the statue of *Moses* (*pl. 32*). A marked likeness appears between the muscular back and shoulders and the contorted, upturned right hand of the Christ Child and the back

view of the figure of *Day* in the Medici Chapel in the Church of San
Lorenzo in Florence. A similar gesture of the upturned hand is used in
the figure of Christ in the *Pietà* (*pl. 34*) of the Cathedral of Florence and
in the figure of *Lorenzo de' Medici* (*pl. 26*) in the Medici Chapel. A bas-
relief in one of the panels of the *Apostles' Doors*, in the bronze doors
designed by Donatello between 1437 and 1443 for the Old Sacristy of the
Church of San Lorenzo in Florence, shows a figure with his right hand
turned upward in the same manner as in the Christ Child. This seems
to be the prototype used by Michelangelo.

The two children on the top landing become the *putti* on the pilas-
ters of the prophets and sibyls in the *Sistine Ceiling* of the Sistine Chapel
in the Vatican. A drawing of a figure in Michelangelo's *Battle of Cascina*
resembles the heavy-legged boy on the steps.

Maternal tenderness is not one of the attributes of the Virgin in
this bas-relief. Her attitude is one of detachment. She appears pensive
rather than melancholy and as if contemplating the tragic events to
come. Vasari writes that Michelangelo expressed the idea that death is
inherent in life and it may well be that the young sculptor had this
thought in mind when he portrayed the boy on the steps, supporting himself with his left hand and holding a drapery or shroud with his right.[20]
At the shoulders of the Virgin and directly opposite the youngster on the
steps is another boy—not too clearly visible as he is sketchily roughed-
out in a faint outline—who appears to be holding the other end of the
shroud.

Much has been written about the spiritual and Neoplatonic implications of the *Madonna of the Stairs*. However, consideration of the
validity of these diverse views and speculations is clearly beyond the
scope of this volume. It is obviously not the purpose of this study to
write an exhaustive, definitive account of every statue. Rather, its aim
is to present a critical analysis of style and content for a better understanding and appreciation of Michelangelo's aesthetic and spiritual
insight which culminated in the *Pietà* of St. Peter's Basilica.

Vasari and Condivi describe the *Battle of the Centaurs* (33.2″ high,
35.6″ wide), but they do not agree on the subject represented. The ico-
nography of the high relief, with its melée of twisting figures, has never
been resolved. That its inspiration is of classical origin is generally
accepted—it undoubtedly stems from Roman sarcophagi decorated with
battle scenes. It was never completed.

Regardless of the story represented, the *Battle of the Centaurs* is
tangible evidence that Michelangelo demonstrated at an early age a

superb knowledge of the human body, a sensitivity for plastic interpretation, a thorough understanding of the mechanics and articulation of fighting figures in violent motion represented in three different planes, and a keen sense of sculptural composition which, all in all, anticipated a successful career in sculpture. It is quite apparent from this early work that the human body was to be Michelangelo's vehicle of artistic creation and invention.

Few sculptors indeed have shown such interesting patterns of light-and-shade, resulting from the juxtaposition of struggling forms, to point up the three-dimensional quality of the figures and the organic unity of the composition. A similar disposition of figures reappears in Michelangelo's *Battle of Cascina* and the *Last Judgment* in the Sistine Chapel.

When Lorenzo died in 1492 at the age of forty-four, Piero de' Medici (1471-1503), his eldest son, became ruler of Florence and Michelangelo returned to his father's home. Sometime later, in January 1494, Piero invited Michelangelo to live at the palace again.[21]

Andrea Cardiere, a musician and lyricist, also lived in Piero's house and was a friend of Michelangelo's. Cardiere had a premonition or hallucination and relates how Lorenzo had appeared to him in black cloak, admonishing him to inform his son, Piero, of the impending expulsion of the Medici from Florence. He revealed his vision to Michelangelo, entreating him to flee from Florence, as he would undoubtedly incur the anger of the enemy—King Charles VIII of France—as a friend of the Medici. Michelangelo counselled Cardiere to tell Piero. Knowing Piero's ugly temper and disposition, Cardiere hesitated, but one day he mustered the courage to inform him. The expected happened. Cardiere was soundly berated, abused and ridiculed.[22] Stricken by fear of the impending disaster, Cardiere and Michelangelo, together with two companions, left Florence for Venice. After a few days they went to Bologna, probably in October 1494.[23]

Condivi's account is somewhat nebulous regarding Michelangelo's sudden departure from Florence. In his biography of Michelangelo he writes that about three years after the death of Lorenzo, the Medici family was exiled.[24] Piero and his family were expelled by the Florentine people on November 9, 1494 for betraying the city to the French sovereign, Charles VIII (1483-1498). Eight days later, on November 17, 1494, King Charles occupied Florence. But the French army, which had been encouraged to remain by Fra Girolamo Savonarola (1452-1498), evacuated the city after ten days; and one year following his invasion of Italy, King Charles was back on French soil. The Medici were not restored to Florence until 1512, and Piero died in exile in 1503. Thus Cardiere's prophecy or vision came true.[25]

King Charles' invasion of Italy to attack the Kingdom of Naples was an adventure he undertook at the instigation of Ludovico Sforza, called "*Il Moro*," ruler of Milan, who feared an attack by Naples. Sforza not only invited King Charles to invade Italy, he also promised him the support of Milan. The French King was not interested in occupying Florence, but he did insist on passing through the city on his way to Naples.[26]

Condivi is apparently in error when he states that Michelangelo was about twenty or twenty-one years of age when Piero and his family were banished from Florence.[27] If this were true, the Medici were then exiled in 1495 or 1496. Documents show, however, that the Medici family was ostracized by an angry populace in November 1494.[28]

Michelangelo remained in Bologna a little more than a year, returning to Florence at the end of 1495. During his stay in Bologna the young sculptor chanced to meet a Bolognese nobleman and art patron, Gianfrancesco Aldovrandi. A prominent man in the civic affairs of Bologna, Aldovrandi invited Michelangelo to live in his house as his guest. It was while he lived with Aldovrandi that Michelangelo devoted himself to the study of Dante, Petrarch and Boccaccio.[29]

Strolling through the city one day, Aldovrandi and Michelangelo stopped at the Church of San Domenico to see the sculptural sepulcher of San Domenico, which had three missing statuettes. Aldovrandi commissioned Michelangelo to complete the sepulcher, and they were executed between the fall of 1494 and the winter of 1495. All three figures are carved in marble: an *Angel* (20.3″), *St. Petronius* (35.2″) and *St. Proculus* (23″).[30]

A newly discovered work of immense importance and interest is the marble statue of *Youthful St. John the Baptist* (*pl. 12 through 14*), which iconographically and stylistically points persuasively to Michelangelo's lost *San Giovannino*. This beautiful statue, in white Carrara marble, was rediscovered about 1900 and is at present in the collection of Piero Tozzi of New York, the well-known art authority, who acquired it in 1942. Condivi and Vasari mention a San Giovannino statue by Michelangelo, but neither biographer gives a description of it.[31]

Condivi reports that a *San Giovannino* was commissioned by Lorenzo di Pierfrancesco de' Medici (1463-1507) in 1495, following Michelangelo's return to Florence from Bologna, and completed in 1496

before the sculptor left for Rome. Chronologically, *Youthful St. John*
appears to have been executed between the three marble statuettes he
carved in Bologna and the *Bacchus (pl. 14)*, which was commissioned
and carved in Rome in 1496.[32]

On June 29, 1497, Paolo Somenzi wrote to the Duke of Milan that
valuable objects from the household of Lorenzo di Pierfrancesco were
being shipped to Mugello, a town near Imola on the southeast border of
Bologna, where Lorenzo went to live to escape the growing enmity of the
Florentines.[33] No doubt this statue was among his valuable possessions.

Significantly, in the latter part of the nineteenth century, a collector
named Albitez discovered the *Youthful St. John* in the region of Bologna.
At that time it was mistakenly attributed to Andrea Sansovino (1460-
1529). In 1900, Daniel Z. Noorian, an American art dealer, purchased
the statue from Albitez and brought it to the United States. Seven years
later an Italian law was enacted prohibiting the exportation of works of
art from Italy. Noorian died in 1930 and the statue remained in the
possession of his widow until 1942, when it was purchased by the present owners, Mr. and Mrs. Piero Tozzi of New York. These are the earliest
known facts of its origin.[34]

San Giovannino or *Youthful St. John the Baptist* is a life-sized figure of an ephebic lad of about twelve or thirteen years of age. The
statue is 41.6 inches in height and 22 inches in width. St. John is seated
on a roughly-cut rock and holds a shell in his right hand; his left hand
grips an edge of the rock for support. He is seated in a *contrappósto*
position with the legs set apart. A sheepskin, fastened by a leather strap
across his chest, hangs from his left shoulder and covers a good part of
his back (*pl. 13*). It is folded casually over his right thigh and across his
groin. Loose locks of hair are gathered over his forehead and fall over
the back of the neck, framing the full, adolescent face. His head is
turned sharply to the right, while his eyes are fixed and stare into the
distance. The Cross St. John customarily carries was originally fitted into
the slender tubular container carved of marble, visible below his left
hand, and held between his thumb and index finger (*pl. 12*). It was of
bronze and is now lost (*pl. 14*). A lamb, an attribute of St. John the Baptist, is shown reclining at the foot of the statue with its head positioned
in the opposite direction to that of St. John.

The lamb was used as a symbol of Christ in the early Christian and
medieval periods and became an attribute of St. John the Baptist in the
Italian Renaissance. Here, the introduction of the lamb probably derives
from Leonardo da Vinci (1452-1519), who was among the first to use

the lamb as a playmate of the Christ Child and St. John in his paintings and drawings. An ancient carved onyx, formerly in the Medici Collection and now in the Archaeological Museum in Florence—*Argus Guarding Jo*—shows a shepherd seated on a rock with a calf lying at his feet.[35] Michelangelo must have known this cameo. His familiarity with the carved gems in the Medici Collection is attested to by Vasari and Condivi. Condivi says that Lorenzo the Magnificent often showed his collection of cameos, intaglios, gems and medallions to Michelangelo and that Piero de' Medici, who succeeded his father in 1492, sent for Michelangelo whenever he wanted to buy carved gems. Thus it is recognized that Lorenzo de' Medici's gem and ancient sculpture collection had a far-reaching influence on Michelangelo's work.[36]

In the painting and sculpture of fifteenth century Florence, St. John the Baptist was often represented as a youth, usually in a standing position. The orientation of Michelangelo's figure toward the antique is clearly shown by his preference for the seated pose, thus relating *Youthful St. John* to the young gods of classical antiquity. There is a striking affinity between the pose of *Youthful St. John* and the various figures of Apollo and Hermes seated on a rock, sometimes playing a musical instrument, the cithara, as seen in Greek Hellenistic and Roman marbles and carved gems known in Michelangelo's day.[37]

The *contrappósto* first noticed in Michelangelo's *Battle of the Centaurs (pl. 9)*, later suggested in the Christ Child of the *Madonna of the Stairs (pl. 10)*, finds its full expression and development in *Youthful St. John*. All of Michelangelo's figures are contained within a *contrappósto* system that is both kinetic and dynamic, creating a superb harmony and balance of all parts. The *contrappósto* organization that unified *Youthful St. John* with its reclining lamb finds a vivid parallel in the god *Bacchus* and the satyr *(pl. 14)*. In the *Pietà* of St. Peter's Basilica, *contrappósto* is more subtly expressed, but it is there all the same. Probably intended for a baptismal font, *Youthful St. John* was designed to be seen from all sides; consequently, there is an awareness of surrounding space and movement. Space and form are brought into effective agreement and this is the genius of Michelangelo.

Michelangelo's *Youthful St. John* abandons the perspective style of fifteenth century reliefs for the more exciting sculpture of the nude figure in-the-round with its rhythmic complex of contours and three-dimensional form. From this moment, the free-standing human figure becomes the principal motif and inspiration of Michelangelo's art.

The writer has had the opportunity to study this impressive statue.

It possesses many parallels of style and workmanship found in other statues by Michelangelo. These similarities and comparisons are descriptively illustrated by a series of photographs in a recent publication by the Italian scholar, Fernanda de' Maffei, in which an abundance of pictorial evidence is presented. The weight of this evidence is overwhelming, offering rational and incontrovertible proof that *Youthful St. John* is an original Michelangelo.

Youthful St. John belongs to the same sculptural tradition as the *Bacchus*, the St. Peter's *Pietà* and the *Bruges Madonna*. They are linked stylistically; all show the same advanced knowledge of human anatomy; the same conception of form; the same spontaneity of execution; the same intuitive and psychological understanding of the theme; the same orientation toward the antique. Moreover, *Youthful St. John* embodies the same elements of Christian spirit and Neoplatonic ideals that filter through the fabric of the *Pietà* in St. Peter's Basilica and the *Bruges Madonna*.

De' Maffei establishes valid and positive affinities, not only with Michelangelo's sculptures, paintings and drawings, but also with the ancient sculpture and carved gems of the Medici Collection. Persuasive and cogent proof is presented detailing the influence this statue had on a number of artists. A drawing by Correggio (Antonio Allegri, 1494-1534) in the Uffizi Gallery in Florence and a Correggio painting of about 1518-1519—now lost but known from a sixteenth century engraving—have figures that are clearly based on the *Youthful St. John*. A 1523 painting of *St. John the Baptist* by Giuliano Bugiardini (1475-1554) in the Pinacoteca of Bologna was also inspired by the same statue. Bugiardini was an old friend of Michelangelo's. They were the same age and were apprenticed in the studio of Domenico Ghirlandaio at the same time. In 1508, Michelangelo invited Bugiardini to assist him in painting the Sistine Ceiling. Later Bugiardini painted a portrait of Michelangelo. Later works—a drawing by Francesco Brizio (1574-1623), a seated nude attributed to Guido Reni (1575-1623)—establish that *Youthful St. John* was seen and admired in the environs of Bologna where the statue was ultimately rediscovered toward the end of the nineteenth century, as previously noted.[38] A drawing of a youth by Michelangelo in the Ashmolean Museum in Oxford contains many similarities to the *Youthful St. John* and is possibly the germ of its conception.

It is significant to bear in mind that except for Michelangelo there was no sculptor on the contemporary scene at the close of the fifteenth century and the beginning of the sixteenth who possessed the creative genius to conceive and execute this beautiful statue of *Youthful St. John*. This fact has never been challenged since its discovery. *Youthful St. John* has all the identification marks and stylistic characteristics of Michelangelo's work. The structure of sculptural motifs, the actual technique, the many details and the general design are Michelangelesque and recur in other statues.

There is no doubt that physical evidences of style are more reliable than literary documentation in the matter of attribution and in the identification of an artist, however valuable and desirable the latter may be. An excellent case in point is the misinformation and incorrect attributions in Vasari's original edition of *Le Vite*. Mistaken attributions have occurred repeatedly in the history of art. In the absence of a drawing or a written description of *Youthful St. John,* the art historian, critic and scholar must turn to the tangible evidence of the artist's work for identification, classification and attribution. Archaeologists have reconstructed accurately entire civilizations of the ancient world by a study of the tangible manifestations of these cultures that have survived the ravages of time. The art historian has been able to make authentic identifications by the same process. And it is by the same systematic procedure and analysis that the *Youthful St. John* has been identified as the work of Michelangelo.

In the carving process, a sculptor develops a technical language that becomes peculiarly his own. Once the nature of this technical language is understood and its characteristics known, it becomes as distinctive as the artist's signature. This kind of physical documentation is of vital importance. And when the attributes of style are considered together with the physical facts, the problems of identification are simplified.

It is the responsibility of the serious scholar to offer verification for a positive attribution of a work of art. This does not necessarily mean that he must rely entirely on the discovery of a letter, a record or other literary sources for a description of the work of art. It means that every possible source of information must be explored and investigated, including the work of art itself. More information may be derived from a work of art than from any other source. This is an incontrovertible dictum. On the other hand, it is also the responsibility of the serious scholar to establish irrefutable proof in defense of an opinion or a disagreement. It is not enough to declare that a statue is a Michelangelo, or that it is not, without proof. An art historian does not serve the aims of scholarship and contributes little when he fails to support his opinion or conviction,

one way or the other, simply by making a declaration without corrobora-
tive facts.

A guiding principle in the evaluation of a work of art is suggested
by two world-renowned art historians and scholars, Bernard Berenson
and Erwin Panofsky. Berenson made the following observation: "The
critic and historian of the work of art, partaking of both the artist's and
the scholar's activities, should start with being as intuitive toward it,
enjoying it as spontaneously, and with as little deliberation, as its creator
who first conceived it. After which only is he called upon to analyze and
interpret, to trace and account for its effects, moral and cultural as well
as artistic." Another relevant statement by Berenson reads: "The trouble
with some art writings, and most so-called aesthetics and treatises on art
in the abstract, is that they seldom if ever betray that the author has
'lived' the work of art. They are the outcome of reading and cogitation.
Their interest is not in the individual work of art, but in the metaphysical
system of which aesthetics is but a *coda* to which it is attached, I sometimes think, as a tin can to a cat's tail." In the same vein, Panofsky
believes: "We would be entirely at a loss were we to depend on the literary sources alone."[39]

The attribution of *Youthful St. John the Baptist* to Michelangelo
grew out of this kind of scholarly probing, inductive analysis and personal experience with the work of art itself, as suggested by Berenson
and Panofsky.

On his return to England, after seeing *Youthful St. John* in New
York in 1956, Sir Kenneth Clark, the distinguished British art critic and
historian, wrote in a letter that he regarded the statue a masterpiece and
was inclined to believe that the hypothesis of its attribution was correct.[40]

With the completion of *Youthful St. John* and with several letters
of introduction from Lorenzo di Pierfrancesco de' Medici, Michelangelo
left for Rome sometime between June 20 and 21, 1496, arriving in the
Eternal City on or about June 25.[41] This was Michelangelo's first visit to
the papal city. On the day of his arrival, he went to call on Cardinal
Raffaele Riario with one of his letters of introduction. The largest collections of antique statuary in Rome were those of Cardinal Riario (housed
in the newly completed Palazzo Riario, now called the Palazzo della
Cancelleria) and Cardinal Giuliano della Rovere, who later became Pope
Julius II (1503-1513).[42] Cardinal Riario invited Michelangelo to inspect
his collection and to give him an opinion. Michelangelo was profoundly
impressed by the beauty of the antique statues and expressed his admi-
ration to the Cardinal.[43]

In Rome, Michelangelo carved a life-size figure of an indulgent *Bacchus* (*pl. 14*), now in the Bargello or the Museo Nazionale in Florence; also a life-size *Apollo* or *Cupid*, now lost. Both statues were acquired by Jacopo Gallo, a Roman nobleman and banker who befriended Michelangelo and became his patron. It was Jacopo Gallo who also arranged the contract for the *Pietà* in St. Peter's Basilica.[44]

Bacchus (Dionysus), the Greek god of wine, was executed in 1496-1497. He is portrayed according to Greek tradition with the usual cup of wine, clusters of grapes and vine leaves in his thick curly hair. The nude god rises from a roughly hewn base and rests against a tree trunk. His eyes are set in a full round face and have the fixed, faraway look of the excessive drinker. A lion's skin partly filled with bunches of grapes hangs from his left hand and a little satyr, sitting on the tree trunk, nibbles at the grapes in childish amusement.

Bacchus' head is turned down and slightly to his right, as if he were trying to maintain his balance. This is a classical figure interpreted in contemporary terms. However, the portrayal of drunkenness and the sensuality of the nude body are not classical. Bacchus lacks the dignity and restraint found in ancient sculptures of the same theme. Both figures twist and turn in a compact spiral composition that leads the observer around the group. The softness of the chest, shoulders and abdomen and the fleshiness of the upper thighs and back are typical of a person who lives a life of self-indulgence, incontinence and excesses. In this respect, Michelangelo represented the true nature of Bacchus. However, it cannot be logically maintained that because of this fleshy softness that the figure of Bacchus is feminine and, consequently, intentionally hermaphroditic.

Vasari described Bacchus in both editions of his *Vite* and refers to its alleged feminine characteristics: *"et particularmente avergli dato la sveltezza della gioventù del maschio, e la carnosità et tondezza della femmina."* Vasari believed that Michelangelo gave the figures the slenderness of the male figure but the fleshiness and roundness of a woman. He estimated that Bacchus was eighteen years old and the satyr about seven. Aldovrandi's description of Bacchus, in his *Delle statue antiche* published in 1556, does not make any reference to hermaphroditic characteristics.

Tolnay suggests that the three heads in the statue of Bacchus are cosmic symbols: the satyr symbolizes the renewal of life; Bacchus represents the decline of life; and the head of the lion skin on the base of the statue between the cleft feet of the satyr signified death.

In the nude figure of Bacchus, Michelangelo was faced with his first real problem of the adult male. It begins his veneration and glorification of the human figure.

The foregoing preamble or precis of Michelangelo's life is intended as a necessary background to the introduction of the critique and discussion of the main subject of this study: the *Pietà*.

· PART TWO ·

Pietà *restates medieval doctrine of Divine Purpose* / *Michelangelo commissioned to carve* Pietà / *Contract for* Pietà / *Origins of the theme* / *Antecedents of Michelangelo's* Pietà / *No parallel to* Pietà / *Aesthetic considerations* / *Christ not portrayed as a cadaver* / *Christ and Madonna a sculptural entity* / *Size of Madonna of the* Pietà / *Design of the* Pietà / *Madonna's youthfulness explained* / *Influence of Neoplatonism on Michelangelo* / *Savonarola's influence on Michelangelo* / *Mary in the* Bruges Madonna

THROUGHOUT HIS LIFE, Michelangelo had been an ardent believer in Christianity and a communicant of the Catholic Church.[45] Without this religious conviction, it is doubtful that he would have been able to create his epic monument and imbue it with such spiritual nobility and divine beauty. Creative genius and religious belief have been fused harmoniously to evoke reverence and veneration. Unless these motivating factors are understood, it is difficult to gain a full appreciation of the qualities, sacred and aesthetic, inherent in the *Pietà*. Only within this context is it possible to measure its greatness.

God made man in His own image; consequently, man is the most beautiful manifestation of God. Man, however, must strive for perfection by elevating his soul and fulfilling his spiritual potential. To attain this perfection, the artist must direct his creative energies towards the exaltation of man's soul and inner being.[46] Michelangelo strove to make man himself the image of the divine and to suggest by the outward form the infinity within. The Neoplatonic doctrine that the body was the outward expression of the soul was fully embraced by Michelangelo.[47]

Michelangelo had boundless faith in God and he was a firm believer in the medieval doctrine of Divine Purpose. His conception of the *Pietà* is a reaffirmation of this doctrine and belief.[48]

French Cardinal Jean de Bilhères de Lagraulas, whom the Italians

called Cardinal di San Dionigi (Saint-Denis), commissioned Michelangelo to carve the *Pietà*. He had been Abbot of Saint-Denis outside of Paris
in 1474 and French Ambassador to the Holy See in Rome under Charles
VIII (1483-1498). He had also served under King Louis XI (1461-1483).
Pope Alexander VI (1492-1503) made him Cardinal of Santa Sabina in
Rome in 1493. He died in Rome on August 6, 1499, before the *Pietà* had
been completed.[49]

On August 27, 1498, a contract was signed between the French
Cardinal and Jacopo Gallo, who served as Michelangelo's agent or representative. The contract not only stipulated the terms and conditions
agreed upon for the execution of the statue, it also showed that Jacopo
Gallo was the guarantor for both the Cardinal and the sculptor. The
contract reads as follows:

Rome, 27 August 1498
Grant to Michelangelo for a marble group of the *Pietà* in Rome.

On the 27th day of the month of August 1498.

B E IT KNOWN AND MANIFEST to all who will read this document that
the Most Reverend Cardinal of Saint-Denis has agreed with mas-
tcr *Michelangelo*, Florentine sculptor, that the said master will make
at his [the Cardinal's] expense, a Pietà in marble, that is a Virgin
Mary clothed, with Christ dead in her arms, as large as a [life-size]
well-proportioned man, for a price of 450 gold ducats of papal coinage, to be paid within one year from the beginning of the work. And
the said Most Reverend Cardinal promises [agrees] to pay in the following manner, that is, to start with, he promises to pay 150 gold
ducats of papal coinage before the work is started, and once the work
is started he agrees to pay 100 ducats of the same coinage to the said
[above mentioned] *Michelangelo* every four months, so that the
afore mentioned 450 gold ducats of papal coinage will be completely
paid in one year, if the said work will be completed; and if the work
will be completed before the year [is over], his Most Reverend Lord-
ship will pay the remainder [balance] at once.

And, I, Iacopo Gallo, guarantee [promise] the Most Reverend
Monsignore that the said *Michelangelo* will complete the said work
within one year and that it will be the most beautiful work in marble
to be seen today in Rome, and that no other master could produce a
better work. And, on the other hand, I guarantee [promise] the said
Michelangelo that the Most Reverend Cardinal will pay in accord-
ance with the above stipulation. And in witness therefore, I, Iacopo
Gallo, have written the present document with my own hand, on the

above inscribed year, month and day. It is understood that this document renders null and void any other such document written by me or by the hand of the above mentioned master *Michelangelo,* and that this agreement is the only valid one.

The Most Reverend Cardinal has given to me, Iacopo, some time ago, 200 gold ducats of Chamber coinage and today 50 gold ducats of papal coinage.

It is so Ioannes, Cardinal S. Dyonisii
I agree to the same Iocobus Gallus,
by his own hand.[50]

In spite of this contract, dated August 27, 1498, there is evidence to support the fact that the statue in question had been started before this contract was made.[51]

The theme of the *Pietà* already existed in Gothic sculpture, both in France and Germany, prior to the fifteenth century. Near the end of the thirteenth century, Gothic sculpture, with its strong religious imagery, felt a need for themes with even greater emotional appeal. This need was fulfilled by the *Pietà* motif with all its emotional intensity, though no such story is found in the Scriptures of the Passion of Christ. Since Germany played a leading part in the development of this theme, it is known by the term, *Andachtsbild,* a devotional image.[52]

An early fourteenth century German *Pietà* in wood, 34.5 inches high, is in the Provinzialmuseum in Bonn. Its purpose is manifestly to arouse a sense of horror and pity in the observer, to enable him to relate his own feelings with the grief of the Virgin.[53] Great reliance is made on the psychological principle of empathy to establish the intended emotional attitude.

In this wooden *Pietà* Christ's emaciated body is shown seated on His mother's lap. He has an oversized head that projects awkwardly into space, and blood is encrusted on His body. Christ's right arm is stretched across the body of His mother.[54] The over-all effect is overwhelmingly grotesque and its emotionalism is not pleasant.

In 1390 a *Pietà* by the sculptor Claus Sluter (active 1375-1405), showing the Virgin with the dead Christ on her lap accompanied by two angels, was in the chapel of the Chartreuse of Champmol. This *Pietà,* which has since been lost, is probably the first recorded one in France.[55] Not until the fourteenth century did Christian art turn by preference to themes such as the *Pietà* and the *Entombment.*[56] Prior to this time the *Pietà* had not been popular in Italy as a religious theme. The author does not agree with Morey when he states that the *Pietà* (c. 1470) from Villeneuve-les-Avignon in the Louvre, Paris, is the finest rendering of the theme in art, not excepting Michelangelo's *Pietà* in St. Peter's in Rome.[57] This painting is contrary to everything Michelangelo believed was the essence of art, painted as it was in a different intellectual climate, in a different culture and in a society with different aspirations. Morey's comparison, in the opinion of the author, does not seem valid.

Literally hundreds of renderings of the Madonna-and-Child, painted or carved by almost every painter and sculptor of the fifteenth century Italian Renaissance, may be the antecedents of Michelangelo's *Pietà*.

In the Madonna-and-Child motifs, the Christ Child sits, stands or lies across the Madonna's lap. He is shown either on the left or right side of His mother. There is a common denominator that binds all these together iconographically: the Madonnas all sit on a throne in the center; their knees or feet are always on the same level; they are always heavily robed. No great transition exists between the Madonna-and-Child theme and the *Pietà*. Basically, the compositions are the same, and one seems to be the counterpart of the other. With a creative genius like Michelangelo, such a transition was obviously not difficult to make. Substituting the dead Christ for the Christ Child requires only a simple change.

Michelangelo disclaimed borrowing ideas from others.[58] Nevertheless, the influence on his work by other painters and sculptors is self-evident and documented. Vasari writes that when Michelangelo used the ideas of others he re-interpreted them so creatively that the original idea was completely transfigured. Panofsky also speaks of Michelangelo's borrowings and creative transformations.[59]

A painting of a Madonna and Child with a motif very similar to Michelangelo's *Pietà* is the *Nativity,* now in the Church of Notre-Dame in Aigueperse, Auvergne, by Benedetto Ghirlandaio.[60] Enthroned before a manger, Benedetto's Madonna is surrounded by many people. The Christ Child is on the Madonna's right. Her left hand is extended away from her body and the palm of the hand is parallel to the picture plane. This is not the same gesture used in Michelangelo's *Pietà*, but it is one of the few Madonnas with her left arm outstretched.

Clements believes that the gesture of the Madonna's left hand in Michelangelo's *Pietà*, and the limp right arm of Christ, were probably suggested by Jacopo dell Sellaio's (c. 1441-1493) painting of the *Pietà* (c. 1483), in the Church of San Frediano, in Florence.[61]

Sellaio's *Pietà* shows Christ on His mother's lap. His head and legs dangle, but Christ's right arm falls away from His body as in Michelangelo's *Pietà*. St. Jerome is on one side and a Bishop Saint, holding Christ's head, is on the other. Until 1945, when it was destroyed, Sellaio's painting was in the Staatliche Museum in Berlin.[62]

Another possible precedent for Michelangelo's *Pietà*, suggested by Tolnay, is the German sculptured *Pietà* in the Church of San Domenico in Bologna, where Michelangelo worked on the sepulchral monument of San Domenico in 1494-1495.[63]

Ercole de' Roberti's (c. 1450-1496) *Pietà* may have been another source of inspiration. This picture by the Ferrara painter was executed for the Church of San Giovanni in Monte in Bologna. And there is a strong likelihood that Michelangelo saw the painting during his stay at Bologna. This painting is now in the Walker Art Gallery, Liverpool. Roberti's Madonna wears an ample mantle and holds the body of Christ without assistance. It is a stiff and awkward figure. Christ's right arm dangles as in Michelangelo's *Pietà*. Christ's head is thrown back and is supported by the Madonna's right hand. She holds Christ's left wrist with her left hand and her head is turned slightly to her right. Three crosses appear on a hill in the distant background. It is a very dramatic representation.[64]

It is reasonable to assume that the French Cardinal chose the theme of the *Pietà* because of its popularity in France. But it does not necessarily follow that Michelangelo was in any way influenced by the manner or stylization in which this theme was treated by French artists. On the contrary, Michelangelo's interpretation of the *Pietà* has no parallel in either France or Germany, where the theme was also well known. In both countries, the *Pietà* group almost always consisted of a small, awkward figure of Christ lying helplessly on His mother's lap. Its main objective, votive and devotional, was to evoke emotional responses to induce the observer to identify himself vicariously with the sufferings of Christ and with the Madonna's grief.

French and German artists portrayed the figure of Christ smaller than life-size and smaller than His mother, with the result that the two figures were not related to each other either in size or design. The imbalance this created was not compatible with Michelangelo's aesthetic sensibility or with his concept of beauty. Michelangelo's *Pietà* is spiritually expressive, well proportioned, heroic in size and monumental in effect. It is only related to French or German interpretations of this theme in subject matter.

It is difficult to agree with Tolnay's hypothesis that the figure of Christ in Leonardo da Vinci's *Last Supper* (1495-1498) explains Michelangelo's triangular composition of his *Pietà*.[65] There is no documented evidence that Michelangelo ever saw Leonardo's painting, though Tolnay suggests that Michelangelo must have seen a drawing or an engraving of the *Last Supper*. This is not incontrovertible proof.[66]

Leonardo's Christ is contained within a simple triangle. It is one element in a geometry of interrelated and interconnected parts. Michelangelo's "triangular" composition is substantive and does not rely or depend on other factors. It is an entity in itself, consisting of a complex of lines and contours, masses and cavities, depressions and bosses, movement and stability, molded harmoniously in a sculptural symphony.

Moreover, the *Pietà* is not a triangular composition, but a pyramidal one. A sculptor thinks in three dimensions, not in two. A triangle is geometrically a two-dimensional flat figure. A pyramid is three dimensional and suggests the compactness of form and design found in the *Pietà*. A statue is intrinsically three dimensional. A painting is flat — depth and space are illusions created by the painter by the manipulations of his pigments. Space and depth, light and shadow, size and shape, mass and volume in painting are simulated. In sculpture all these elements are real.

Perhaps it would have been more convincing to suggest that the figure of the Virgin in Leonardo's unfinished *Adoration of the Magi* (1481-1482), in the Uffizi Gallery, Florence, influenced Michelangelo. Here the Virgin is placed majestically in the center and encircled by a group of people. She holds the Christ Child on her lap, with her left arm around His body for support. Like Michelangelo's *Pietà*, one foot of the Virgin is placed higher than the other; consequently, one knee is raised higher, as in the *Pietà*. Both Madonnas are turned slightly to one side and both are compact in arrangement and in the disposition of the figures. If Leonardo's Madonna and Child in this painting were reversed, its composition would approximate the position of Michelangelo's group.

In the opinion of the author, the work of Luca della Robbia (1400-1482) is more directly related to Michelangelo's *Pietà* than Leonardo's figure of Christ in the *Last Supper*. Like Michelangelo, Luca was a Florentine sculptor who had mastered the traditions of his time. Luca's two high reliefs of the Madonna and Child bear a striking affinity in design to Michelangelo's *Pietà*. One is the *Madonna of the Rose Garden* in the Bargello in Florence; the other is the *Madonna Frescobaldi* in the Kaiser-Friedrich Museum in Berlin.[67] In both groups, Luca shows the

7. Pietà. *As it appears above eye level.*

8. Pietà. *Detail of the right side.*

OVERLEAF:

6. La Cappella della Pietà, *St. Peter's Basilica, Rome.*

9. Battle of the Centaurs,
1490-1492. *Casa Buonarroti,
Florence.*

10. Madonna of the Stairs, *c. 1491. Casa
Buonarroti, Florence.*

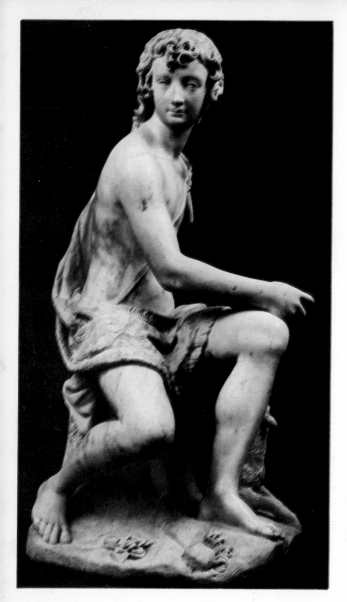

11. Youthful St. John the Baptist, 1496.
Piero Tozzi Collection, New York.

12. Youthful St. John the Baptist, 1496. *Piero Tozzi
Collection, New York.*

14. Bacchus, 1496-1497. *Museo Nazionale, Florence.*

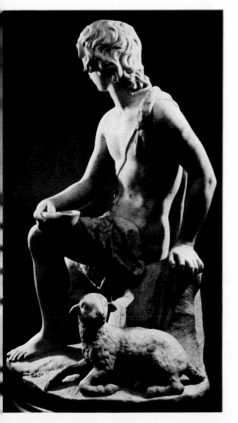

13. Youthful St. John the Baptist, 1496. *Piero Tozzi Collection, New York.*

15. Pietà. *View of the right side.*

16. Pietà. *Detail of Christ's head.*

17. Pietà. *Detail of Christ's body.*

18. Pietà. *Detail of the left side.*

19. Pietà. *Detail of Madonna's head.*

20. Pietà. *Detail of Christ's right hand.*

21. Pietà. *Detail of Christ's right foot.*

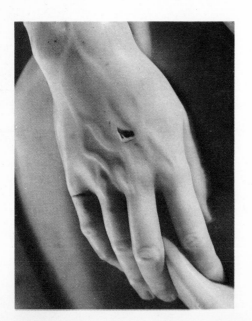

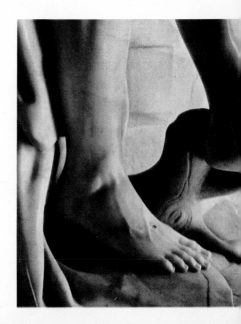

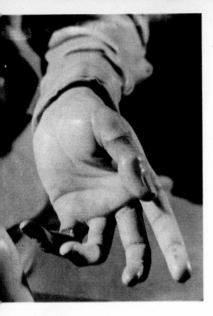

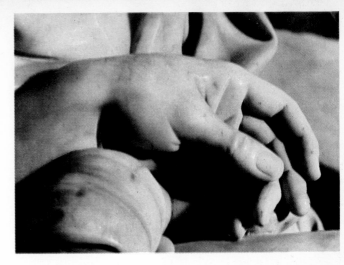

23. Pietà. *Detail of Christ's left hand.*

22. Pietà. *Detail of Madonna's left hand.*

24. Pietà. *As it appears at eye level in St. Peter's Basilica.*

25. Giuliano de' Medici, c. 1553. *Medici Chapel, Church of San Lorenzo, Florence.*

26. Lorenzo de' Medici, c.
1553. *Medici Chapel, Church
of San Lorenzo, Florence.*

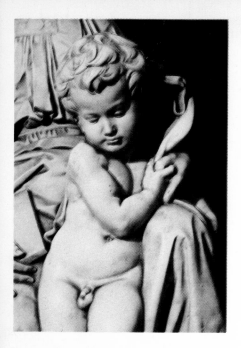

27. Bruges Madonna, *1501-1504.* *Detail of Christ Child. Church of Notre-Dame, Bruges.*

28. Pietà. *Detail of Madonna's face.*

29. Bruges Madonna, *1501-1504. Detail of Madonna's face. Church of Notre-Dame, Bruges.*

30. Pietà. *Detail showing Michelangelo's name inscribed on* cintura *or* band.

31. Bruges Madonna, 1501-1504. Church of Notre-Dame, Bruges.

32. Moses, *1513-1516. Church of*
San Pietro in Vincoli, Rome.

33. Pietà. *Statue showing the two bronze angels
and halo before their removal in 1927.*

34. Pietà. *1548-1555. Cathedral of Florence.*

35. Pietà. *Detail of Christ's body.*

seated Madonna holding the Christ Child on her lap. In both instances, the Madonna is supporting the Child by holding her hand under the Child's armpit, with her arm around His shoulders. This same gesture is found in Michelangelo's *Pietà*, even to the spreading of the Madonna's fingers. It is interesting to observe that both Madonnas, heavily clothed in loose-fitting mantles, have their legs set far apart and that the *Madonna Frescobaldi* has one foot placed considerably higher than the other, paralleling with almost exact faithfulness the Madonna in Michelangelo's *Pietà*.

Luca's two Madonnas, in glazed terra cotta, are resolved in simple triangular compositions in three dimensions, a geometric formula observed by Tolnay and others in Michelangelo's *Pietà*.[68] Michelangelo must have known both statues. To a creative innovator like himself, it was simple indeed to transpose the figures in Luca's two Madonnas to arrive at his own *Pietà*. While Luca's statues are of modest dimensions — the *Madonna Frescobaldi* is 33.8″ high and 23.1″ wide; the *Madonna of the Rose Garden* is 32.6″ high and 24.8″ wide — they contain the fertile seed which, in the writer's opinion, flowered into Michelangelo's *Pietà*.[69]

Donatello's seated figure of *St. John the Evangelist* (1408-1415), in the Museo dell' Opera del Duomo, Florence, 82.6″ high, should not be overlooked as a possible source from which Michelangelo may have obtained his idea for the design of the *Pietà*. It has the same monumental quality and pyramidal composition as the *Pietà*.[70]

Actually, there is no direct iconographic antecedent for Michelangelo's *Pietà* in the entire fourteenth and fifteenth centuries. It is the largest sculpture of its kind anywhere. It is unique, heroic, original and stands alone as a colossus without peer. Michelangelo rejected the rigid portrayals of Christ by his predecessors and contemporaries, in their rendition of the *Pietà* theme, as incompatible with his aesthetic sensibility. In an age of truth, nurtured by the revival of learning which began even prior to the Italian Renaissance, he found it difficult to reconcile the physical facts of a corpse with the beauty of the human body. It was out of this concern that Michelangelo endowed his figure of Christ with lifelike attributes and articulation.

A dead Christ calls for a rigid and angular interpretation to simulate the stiff and inert physical condition of a cadaver. This idea, however, was not in harmony with Michelangelo's creative instincts, particularly since he believed that the human body was God's greatest creation and that divine beauty could be achieved only through this God-made vehicle. Michelangelo did not believe in the exact imitation

of nature, even though he studied it scientifically. Perhaps the only way
to appreciate and understand why Michelangelo represented Christ as
he did was that his highest allegiance was to beauty rather than to
scientific truth. Michelangelo's belief—as revealed in his art and poetry
—that divine beauty is best expressed through the nobility of the human
body is manifested in his *Pietà* group.[71]

To justify his interpretation, Michelangelo did not represent Christ
dead, but portrayed Him at the ebb of His life, or before death. Aesthetic
considerations had to take precedence over historical accuracy. The fact
that Christ was dead when He was taken down from the Cross did not
deter Michelangelo from pursuing an ideal, creative conception. Literary and historical truths are irrelevant when they interfere with or sub-
vert the aesthetic intention of the artist. This aesthetic license is the
artist's prerogative.

Another reason Christ is represented as a living being in the *Pietà*
is dictated by problems of design: if Michelangelo had depicted a corpse,
convention would have required him to show a stiff, inflexible and rigid
body, in the tradition of less imaginative artists. Rigidity does not lend
itself to creative or expressive interpretation. A graceful cadaver would
be an incongruous and unnatural repudiation of its physical nature or
its reality. By portraying Christ before death Michelangelo was able to
create a beautiful and rhythmic composition of great forcefulness. It
should be understood clearly that Michelangelo's Christ is not dead. A
diagnostic examination of the figure will prove this beyond any doubt.

It is not easy to understand why art historians, generation after
generation, have repeated this error. Unfortunately, historians too often
look at works of art through the printed pages of other scholars, rather
than through personal study and analysis, relying on their own eyes,
knowledge and sensibilities. Panofsky once said that you cannot rely
on literary sources alone in the evaluation of a work of art, but this les-
son has not been generally learned.[72]

The origin of the legend that Christ in Michelangelo's *Pietà* is dead
is found in Vasari's *Vite*, repeated by Condivi in his biography of Michelangelo, and perpetuated by almost every art historian since that time.[73]
This is what Vasari wrote:

> *Fra le cose bello vi sono, oltra i panni divini suoi, si scorge il
> morto Cristo; e non si pensi alcuno di bellezza di membra e d' artifi-
> cio di corpo vedere uno ignudo tanto ben ricerci di muscoli, vene,
> nerbi sopra l'ossatura di quel corpo, nè ancora un morte più simile
> al morto di quello.*

Among the beautiful things, that are to be noticed, besides the divine draperies, is the dead Christ; and as far as beauty of members [limbs] and arrangement of the body, no one should expect to see either another nude so thoroughly studied in so far as muscles, veins, and sinews on the bone structure of that body, nor a dead man more like a dead body than that one.

Vasari set the thinking pattern for art historians who continually hold that Michelangelo's Christ is a corpse. This was the assumption of artists of the late fourteenth and fifteenth centuries who painted or carved this theme. Christ's body—rigid, angular, stiff—was usually placed horizontally across the Virgin's lap, and His head and feet were supported by saints. By this stiffness, ungainliness and awkwardness the artist conveyed the idea that Christ was dead. This concept was generally accepted because the people had some acquaintance with the physical characteristics of a cadaver.

In Michelangelo's *Pietà*, visual and physical evidence does not support Vasari's statement that Christ is dead. Careful analysis shows—and the author's thesis is upheld by competent medical authority—that Michelangelo's Christ is still alive.[74]

Pathologists and anatomists consulted by the author agree that the superficial veins on the back forearm in the dangling right arm (*pl. 4, 7*) are usually collapsed in a corpse—here they are engorged, or congested with blood. This arm is also positioned. It should hang limp, perpendicular to the marble base. This is especially so because the right hand of the Madonna is in the right armpit (axilla) supporting Christ's weight, which would normally permit the arm to hang freely.

Christ's right hand is shown clasping a fold of the mantle between the parted second and third fingers (*pl. 20*). The fingers of a dead person do not part. This observation is also applicable to Christ's left hand (*pl. 23*). Actually, the muscles of the hand remain rigid for a long time and assume a clawlike configuration, somewhat like Christ's left hand, unless shaped by someone preparing the body for burial or wake. The veins in the right hand are too conspicuous. A person who dies from shock and hemorrhage, as Christ did, should have had collapse of the peripheral veins.

Perhaps the most conspicuous evidence that the body portrayed was living is the muscular control evidenced in the lower extremities. There is no rigidity or flaccidity. Muscles appear to be under complete control, firmly planted and maintained in a studied position. The position assumed is not a strained or fixed one, but rather one that is controlled, yet relaxed. If the body had lost its rigidity, the lower limbs would show a greater sag (*pl. 18, 24*). If rigidity were still present, they would not appear so relaxed.

Enlargement of the superficial veins of the back (dorsum) of the right foot is another indication of life (*pl. 21*). More contraction is shown in the upper abdominal muscles (rectus) than is generally found in a cadaver. Too well defined for a dead body are the (serratus anterior) muscles of the right chest (thorax) (*pl. 4, 17, 35*). Muscles in a corpse are flaccid, not distended. Another sign of life is shown in the back (tibialis posterior) of the left ankle and the tendon of the medial hamstring muscles of the same leg. In the right leg the calf (peroneal) muscles and the tendon of biceps of the thighbone (femur) do not suggest a dead body.

The expression of the face is one of peace, quiet and restfulness (*pl. 3, 8, 16, 17*). The face of a corpse is expressionless. This is not true of Christ's face. He appears to be in a serene, peaceful sleep. There is no evidence of pain or scourging, except for the nail holes in His hands and feet and the wound on the right side of His chest. In death the eyelids are open, fixed and inanimate. Christ's eyelids are gently closed. The lower jaw of a cadaver is usually fixed and rigid; the lips invariably parted, expressionless and formless, and the mucous membrane covering them is dry and dull in appearance. On the contrary, Christ's lips are parted, beautifully shaped, and seem almost ready to speak. Anyone who died the agonizing death of Christ would have had his face covered with dried sweat and blood clots.

Soon after death, the body becomes rigid. This is called post-mortem rigidity and is caused by the hardening of the muscular tissues. Rigidity disappears from one to six days after death, or when decomposition begins. It is possible that Michelangelo may have represented Christ at this stage, except that the body loses all its muscle tone, becomes completely flaccid, and sags if it is not supported. These physical characteristics, however, are not present in the figure of Christ. The only indication of death may be the position of Christ's head, which has fallen back over the arm of the Virgin (*pl. 8, 15, 16*).

Michelangelo was well aware of the visual and physical aspects of a corpse as well as the manifestations of life when he chose to interpret his "dead" Christ. No one disputes his thorough knowledge of human anatomy. In fact, Vasari and Condivi record in their biographies of Michelangelo how devotedly he dissected cadavers to increase his knowledge of the skeletal structure and the musculature of the body.

Michelangelo knew the origin and insertion of every topographical or superficial muscle of the body, and his statues and paintings are ample evidence of this knowledge. A thorough understanding of human anatomy is essential to a sculptor.

Vasari relates that Michelangelo carved a wooden crucifix for the Prior (Maestro Nicholaio di Giovanni di Lapo Bichiellini) of Santo Spirito in Florence. Santo Spirito is a church, monastery and hospital with a mortuary.[75] In gratitude the Prior provided the young sculptor with a room to dissect cadavers. Condivi writes that Michelangelo applied himself with such zeal and diligence and for such long periods of time in his dissections that the stench of the decaying bodies made him so sick that he was unable to eat ar drink.[76]

Michelangelo chose to portray Christ before death because good sculptural design dictated that both figures in the *Pietà* had to be resolved into a single unit and the pyramidal form was chosen for its intrinsic compactness and monumentality. Both figures rise from a wide oval base (*pl. 5, 7*). Mary's head, turned slightly to her right, is bowed gently and with compassion toward her Son and forms the apex of the pyramid. Her torso is not in a frontal position but is turned subtly to her right side, and her left shoulder is slightly lower than the right. Had Michelangelo's statue been properly set on its present base in the Cappella della Pietà (*pl. 6, 7*), the Madonna's left shoulder would have been considerably lower and Christ's face more visible. For unknown reasons the statue was raised on a wedge-shaped base and tilted to the left.

Michelangelo used the full dimensions of the original block of white Carrara marble for the figures, leaving a rather thin marble base. Redig de Campos illustrates this point in a scholarly article published in 1963.[77] It is apparent that Michelangelo did not intend the *Pietà* to be seen in the tilted position mentioned. Recent reports indicate that this situation will be corrected when the *Pietà* is returned to St. Peter's Basilica at the close of the New York World's Fair.

Mary's two arms are brought forward; her right arm is stretched across the back of Christ's shoulders, and the hand, reaching with spread fingers, is held securely under His armpit, supporting Him and holding Him to her bosom. From a frontal view (*pl. 1*), the imaginary diagonal created by her head, left arm and Christ's left leg forms one side of the pyramid.

To provide an adequate base and a proper setting for the reclining body of Christ, Michelangelo clothed the Virgin in an excessively voluminous and loose-fitting cloak. This necessary device gives stability and balance to the entire sculptural ensemble, enhances its monumental effect, and creates the pleasing psychological assurance that the Madonna is physically able to bear the weight of her Son without difficulty.

It would have been disastrous aesthetically if the figure of Christ had not been silhouetted against a solid background. Except for the protrusion of the left leg, the Madonna provides the background for Christ's entire body. To provide this adequate base for the figure of Christ, Michelangelo made the group wider than it is high. The *Pietà* has an overall height of 68.5″ and its width is 76.7″, a difference of almost nine inches.

To balance Christ's body effectively Michelangelo spread the knees of the Madonna apart and placed them at different levels to create a valley into which Christ's body is cradled. He rests in a natural position on Mary's two legs, or lap, and is partly supported by her right arm, extended around the back of His shoulders. Her hand is tucked under Christ's arm, over which His head has fallen. Except for His right hand, Christ's hip is the closest part of His body to the observer. From this point, Christ's body moves back and upward towards the Virgin's shoulder, while both legs recede into the space on the opposite side of the Madonna. The limb of a dead tree-trunk (*pl. 18, 21*) provides a resting place for His left foot. But the body itself, from the lower abdomen to the head, and from the hips to the knees, moves obliquely in space. Christ's two feet are further back than His knees (*pl. 18*).[78]

Christ's back is arched and His body is bent at the neck, waist and knees. Viewing the statue from all sides will disclose that Michelangelo arched the figure of Christ around the front of the Madonna's body and that, basically, Christ's body is conceived within a sweeping arc that begins at His head and swings down and around the Madonna (*pl. 4, 18, 35*). The universal oneness that exists between every mother and child is manifest here in terms of attitude and sculptural design.

Many scholars maintain that the figure of Christ is unnaturally small and that Michelangelo may have been influenced by French *Pietàs* or Northern German *Vesperbilder*, which traditionally, as already noted, used a small under-life-size figure for Christ.[79]

One of the precedents cited for Tolnay for Michangelo's *Pietà* is the German carving of a *Pietà* in the Church of San Domenico, Bologna, where Michelangelo had worked in 1494-1495.[80] Facts, however, do not support the theory that the body of Christ in Michelangelo's *Pietà* is under life-size or unnaturally small. Careful measurements of this figure by the author indicate clearly that the sculptor fulfilled the conditions of his contract with French Cardinal Jean de Bilhères de Lagraulas, which stipulated that the figure of Christ was to be *"grande sia vno homo isuto,"* or "as large as a well-proportioned man."[81]

What makes Christ appear small is the fact that the Madonna is heroic in size. Her body is considerably larger than that of a normal woman. In her seated position, the Madonna is less than four inches under six feet.[82] Standing, she would be about seven feet tall. This explains why Christ appears small, though His proportions are life-size.

Though the figure of the Madonna is larger than life, her head is of natural proportions and, therefore, small in relation to the size of her body. Two purposes were served in making the head life-size: a small head gives the illusion that the body is larger than it is; and a small head was necessary to establish the proper relationship with the head of Christ. If the scale of Mary's head had been in proportion to her body, it would have been larger than life and, consequently, larger than Christ's head. Such a disparity in the size of the two heads would have been aesthetically incongruous and visually unpleasant.

Michelangelo made the Madonna of heroic size with deliberate purpose, but he was also careful not to make her head in the same proportions. The two heads are so close together that it was essential to render them in the same natural proportions. Mary's life-size head thus serves a twofold aesthetic function. Michelangelo must have had knowledge of the fact that a small head makes the body look larger than it really is. Greek sculptors of the fourth century B.C. knew this fact and used it in their work. The *Hermes* (c. 350 B.C.) in Olympia by Praxiteles of Athens and the *Agias* (337 B.C.) in Delphi by Lysippus of Sicyon—two standing nude figures—are examples in point. The same psychological principle is illustrated in the Madonna of the *Pietà,* whose head is life-size to emphasize the proportions of her body, yet it is in perfect agreement in its relationship to the head of Christ. Imagine how bizarre and absurd this statue would have been if Michelangelo had made the Madonna's head larger than that of Christ.

Michelangelo painted many figures with small heads in his frescoes in the *Sistine Ceiling* (1508-1512) and in the *Last Judgment* (1536-1541). Both frescoes are in the Sistine Chapel in the Vatican.

A comparison between the Madonna of the *Pietà* with Michelangelo's seated figures of *Giuliano de' Medici* (1478-1516), Duke of Nemours *(pl. 25),* and *Lorenzo de' Medici* (1492-1519), Duke of Urbino (*pl.* 26), in the Medici Chapel of the Church of San Lorenzo, Florence, will help establish an understanding of the enormous size of the Madonna.

Giuliano was the son and Lorenzo was the grandson of Lorenzo *Il Magnifico*. Both statues were completed before 1533. It is not known definitely which one was executed first and when the work on the two seated figures began. The posture of Giuliano follows closely Michelangelo's painting of the *Prophet Joel* (1509) in the *Sistine Ceiling;* and another prototype is the colossal figure of *Moses* (1513-1516) (*pl.* 32), in the Church of San Pietro in Vincoli, Rome. The bent wrist in the figure of Lorenzo was also used in the Christ Child of the *Madonna of the Stairs* (*pl.* 10), in the Casa Buonarroti, Florence; in the figure of Adam (1511) in the *Creation of Adam,* in the *Sistine Ceiling;* and in the dead Christ in the *Pietà* (1548-1555) (*pl.* 34), in the Cathedral of Florence.

Giuliano and *Lorenzo* are two powerful and full-grown men – the Madonna is a young girl of about sixteen or seventeen. (Michelangelo did not portray her in her true chronological age.) But in spite of her youthfulness, Mary is 68.5″ in height in her seated position, while *Giuliano* is 68.1″ and *Lorenzo* is 70″.[83] This comparison of Mary with the two mature figures of *Giuliano* and *Lorenzo* (*pl.* 24, 25, 26) is the most convincing evidence that Michelangelo deliberately predetermined that the Madonna had to be a towering figure to bring her in proper aesthetic relationship with the figure of Christ. There seems to be little doubt that the problem of balance and design motivated Michelangelo to make Mary larger than the figure of Christ.

The reader should attempt to visualize a life-size woman struggling to balance a full-grown man of thirty-three (the age Christ died) on her lap, to realize the necessity of making the Madonna as large as Michelangelo conceived her.

Mary's heroic-size figure creates a better sculptural relationship between the two figures, and avoids the incongruity of the figure of Christ dwarfing that of His mother and overhanging grotesquely on either side of her, in the tradition of the fourteenth century. By enlarging the dimensions of Mary to heroic proportions, Michelangelo made the Madonna's task of supporting the weight of Christ's body seem plausible. Michelangelo presumably saw the two figures as a simple harmonious entity which could be achieved only by making the figure of the Madonna larger than life.

As a Neoplatonist, Michelangelo believed that the proportions or conception of a work of art are determined by its own aesthetic needs.

This did not spare him from unjustified criticism and condemnation.[84]

A copy of Michelangelo's *Pietà,* carved by Nanni di Baccio Bigio, was given as a gift in 1549 to the Church of Santo Spirito in Florence. This prompted an unidentified writer, in a letter of March 19, 1549, to slander Michelangelo for subverting faith by the Lutheran ideas expressed in his figure of Christ and accusing him of being the source of filth and obscenity in art. The writer apparently believed that the "small" figure of Christ was an expression of Lutheran ideas because it purported to follow the tradition of German sculpture.[85] The same writer was also critical of a nude *Adam and Eve* in the same church.

The *Pietà* is not the only instance in which Michelangelo deliberately distorted the proportions of the human body to attain a greater aesthetic expressiveness. Controlled distortion is found in almost all his sculptures and paintings. But the psychological motivation for this distortion or stylization is not always the same.

The drapery below the figure of Christ is handled with depth and breadth in loose and graceful folds. This is not true of the many little folds, all properly subordinated to the anatomical structure of the Madonna, covering the upper part of her body. Diagonally across her bosom is a band or ribbon on which Michelangelo inscribed his name in Latin: MICHAEL-AGELVS BONAROTVS FLORENT FACIEBAT (*pl.* 30). This is the only statue signed by Michelangelo.

MICHAEL·AGELVS·BONAROTVS·FLOEN·FACIEBAT

Vasari relates how several travelers from Lombardy visited St. Peter's Basilica in Rome and stopped to admire Michelangelo's *Pietà*—which the visitors ascribed to Cristoforo Solari (d. 1527) of Milan, called *"il Gobbo,"* the hunchback. Michelangelo either heard or was informed of this incident and subsequently carved his name across the diagonal band. It is more likely that he signed his name with full realization that this statue represented the zenith of his accomplishments and he proudly inscribed his name upon it.[86]

Tolnay believes that the diagonal band or *cintura* was used by mothers to support their infant babies. It has also been used in paintings of the Madonna and Child, presumably for the same purpose. An example is Fra Filippo Lippi's (c. 1406-1469) *Madonna Enthroned*

(1444) in the Louvre.[87] Michelangelo used a similar band in his drawing of St. Anne in Oxford. Tolnay is convinced that Leonardo da Vinci's Christ in his Last Supper, which has a band across His chest, had a strong influence on Michelangelo's design for the Pietà.[88] The author does not share this view.

The dominant curve, formed by two bold folds of the Madonna's mantle in the front foreground of the statue, is repeated by the position of Christ's right arm. Together they engender a dynamic motion which leads the eye upward to Christ's head. This movement continues to Mary's right shoulder, follows around to the opposite side and descends along her left arm and outward toward the observer. This subtle curve, beginning as it does at the foot of the statue, swings upward, back, around and forward to circumscribe the two figures, welding them together in a powerful and stirring composition. The element of line in this group is as important as the creative handling of mass.

In spite of the Madonna's outstretched arm and the flexing of Christ's knee to extend His left leg, the Pietà is essentially a closed sculpture, compact in form and design, and containing few empty spaces or negative elements. Nevertheless, the sweeping movement triggered by the curved lines of the drapery is not confined to a flat plane but accelerates in three-dimensional space, twisting and turning around the whole group. By guiding the observer's eye through space, Michelangelo achieves a superb effect. Consequently, in designing this statue, he was well aware of the surrounding space—not in the baroque sense—enveloping both figures, which he molded effectively in the same way that he fashioned the solid volumes. Space is everywhere. What is done with it and how it is used depends on the aesthetic motivation or intention of the artist.

While the group is calm and reposeful and the atmosphere one of tranquillity and sorrow, the contours are kinetic and dynamic. A balance is established in this statue between mood and movement—the former peaceful and resigned, the latter spirited and alive. Christ's body is relaxed and graceful, and it is attractively contrasted against the drapery. It was carved with delicacy and care and was given a strong tactile quality and a high-polish finish. Subtle nuances of light and shadow heighten the sculptural qualities of the entire group (pl. 1, 7, 18, 24, 35).

Christ's aristocratic face and high forehead have sharp contours and a clean-cut silhouette (pl. 3, 16, 17). The triangular head is reminiscent of Andrea del Verrocchio's (1435-1488) head of Christ in his bronze statue of Christ and St. Thomas (1465-1483) in the Church of Or San

Michele in Florence—a statue celebrated for its high moral, spiritual and intellectual tone.[89] His hair is parted in the center and falls casually on His mother's arm and on either side of His head to frame the face (*pl. 3, 15*). The hair is rendered in irregular wavy patterns with drill-holes to give it color by producing shadows of different sizes and shapes. A thin mustache and beard curl in little ringlets and cling closely to the bone structure of the face. Partly closed eyelids, a fine nose, beautifully shaped mouth, full and slightly parted lips showing His front teeth, and the strong curve of the eyebrows are treated with sensitivity and tenderness. Christ's slender thighs and legs are portrayed with life-like elegance; the muscles and sinews are well defined and handsomely formed (*pl. 18, 35*).

Adolfo Venturi, the venerated art historian and scholar, described the legs of the dead Christ by this contradictory statement: "his limbs, worked on the turner's lathe, shine with manly beauty."[90] It is difficult to reconcile this derogatory remark that Christ's legs were turned on a lathe—in other words, machine made—with their "manly beauty."

The right foot of Christ (*pl. 21*) bears a striking resemblance to one of the feet of Holofernes in Donatello's bronze, *Judith Slaying Holofernes* (1455), in Florence.[91]

Mary's expression is one of sublime resignation (*pl. 2, 19, 28*). Sorrow and pathos are defined with classic restraint and dignity. Her grief is more than a portrayal of anguish, it is a symbol of Christ's sacrifice for the sins of man and a prophecy of the salvation of all humanity. She bows her head toward Christ with partly closed eyes and with tenderness; and her outstretched, open-hand gesture is an expression of resignation that God's will be done. Four fingers of this hand were broken—they were restored in 1736 by Giuseppe Lironi (*pl. 22*).[92] Records do not show when Christ's small finger on His right hand was broken or restored (*pl. 20*).

The Madonna's long, oval head, with soft cheeks and delicate chin, reveal her youthfulness. A head veil covers part of her forehead; gathered folds, in a variety of shapes, fringe her face and form the neckline of her mantle. The part of the mantle covering her head falls loosely to her shoulders to frame her exquisite features. Mary's full lips are pressed gently together; her straight nose has a slight upward turn at the end.

In his glorification of the Madonna, Michelangelo gives her a nobility of mind and spirit that transcends any pensiveness or melancholy. Michelangelo's idealization of the Madonna, endowed with eternal youth, was severely criticized by his contemporaries. The Mother of Christ had never been represented as a young girl of about sixteen years. Prior to Michelangelo's *Pietà*, painters and sculptors depicted the Madonna as a mature woman. Michelangelo himself used this conventional type in his painting of the *Holy Family* (c. 1504), also known as the *Doni Madonna*, in the Uffizi Gallery, Florence. But for his *Pietà*, he sought a new idealization, a new concept, universal in its implications and embodying his own spiritual feelings.

In the *Pietà* of St. Peter's Basilica and in the *Bruges Madonna* (pl. 31) in the Church of Notre-Dame, Bruges, Michelangelo glorifies a youthful queen whose freshness and innocence are marks of her purity and chastity. Her youth shocked his contemporaries, who regarded it as unworthy and sacrilegious for an artist to deviate from accepted tradition. Michelangelo ignored the criticism that his Madonna was too young in contrast to her dead Son, who died at the age of thirty-three and whom Michelangelo portrayed with due regard to His chronological age. His critics did not understand the sculptor's new and venerated concept of the Virgin Mary.

Condivi one day asked the young Florentine sculptor why he had represented the Madonna so young. Condivi reported the sculptor's explanation in his biography of Michelangelo:

> Do you not know that chaste women maintain their fresh [or youthful] appearance much longer than those who are not? How much more so this would be in a virgin, never even touched by the slightest impurity of [carnal] desire, which might have altered her appearance? I would add moreover that it is credible that this freshness and bloom [flower] of youth, besides being maintained in her by such natural means, were fostered [aided] by the work of God [the Divine] in order to give proof to the world of the virginity and perpetual [eternal] purity of the Mother. This however was not necessary in the Son: rather the contrary, in order to show that the Son of God might actually take on, as he did, a true human body and be subjected to all that an ordinary man undergoes, with the exception of sin; there was no need to restrain by divine means what was human in him, but rather to allow it to follow a natural course and order so that He might look as old as He was. You need not marvel therefore if, for this reason, I made the most Holy Virgin, Mother of God, in comparison to her Son, seem much younger than her real age would require, and I represented the Son His own age.[93]

Michelangelo's explanation was that it was his intention to symbolize the perfect chastity and purity of Mary by immortalizing her youthfulness, and in this way distinguish her from all other women.[94]

Michelangelo strove to make man himself the image of the divine and to suggest by the beauty of the body the infinity within it. He agreed with the Neoplatonic belief that the body was the outward expression of the soul. This thought is reflected in his interpretation of the Madonna. In his glorification of man he transcends the limits of humanity to seek a universal reality beyond man himself.[95]

Michelangelo was influenced, as previously noted, by the Florentine Neoplatonists, Marsilio Ficino and Giovanni Pico della Mirandola, the two leading scholars of the Platonic Academy. Both Platonists remained faithful members of the Catholic Church, as did Michelangelo. Ficino entered the priesthood in 1475 and performed his duties as a parish priest until his death in 1499.[96] It should not be overlooked that the principal inspiration of Ficino and Pico was religious and in intention definitely Christian. This was the influence that had made its mark on Michelangelo when, as a youth, he enjoyed the hospitality of Lorenzo de' Medici's palace where he lived and where he met the great men of letters and scholars of his time.[97]

Another influence on Michelangelo's life was that of the Dominican Friar, Girolamo Savonarola. Condivi says that Michelangelo always had a great love for the reformer and preacher. Between 1490 and 1498, the year of the latter's execution, a large segment of the Florentine people looked to the Friar for guidance in matters of morality and religion. He believed it was his mission to denounce corruption, free men of evil and reform the Church. His enemies, however, tortured him into admitting that he was a heretic and he was hanged and subsequently destroyed by fire for his sins.[98]

His influence on Michelangelo was moral and spiritual. There is no evidence that this influence shaped his art in any way. Savonarola was not in sympathy with the humanists or with the intellectual climate of fifteenth century Florence. He believed that the main function of art was didactic or to teach moral principles.[99]

Michelangelo was a profound believer in Christian faith. However, he was also a humanist and Neoplatonist and did not share Savonarola's views on art. This is demonstrated by his pagan and nude figures of *Bacchus* (*pl. 14*) and *Cupid*, carved during the period of Savonarola's greatest fervor and influence. These would seem to indicate that the Friar's condemnation of physical beauty had little effect on Michelangelo.

The Greeks idealized their gods and strove to attain physical beauty above any other quality in their art. Michelangelo's idealization of the Virgin Mary grew out of his conviction that the human body is God's most beautiful creation. By fusing the Greek concept of beauty with the Neoplatonic belief that man is endowed with an inner vision and spirituality, Michelangelo demonstrated the compatibility of classical ideals and Christian thought. The expression of this compatibility was one of the principal programs and interests of the Neoplatonists of the fifteenth and sixteenth centuries and those artists who came under their influence.

Panofsky writes that among all his contemporaries, Michelangelo was the only one among the artists who genuinely understood and adopted Neoplatonism. And in the judgment of his contemporaries and followers, Michelangelo and classical antiquity had become equivalent.[100] Thus the two greatest motivating forces in his life and in his art were Christianity and Neoplatonism, which he amalgamated to create works of great beauty, both spiritual and aesthetic. Beauty to him was an expression of the divine, and this deep-rooted religious feeling undoubtedly inspired the *Pietà* in St. Peter's Basilica.

Inherent in his reasons for the youthful Madonna is the fact that Michelangelo also exercised his prerogative as an artist in his desire to differentiate between the immortal and the mortal. Michelangelo chose to show Mary's sanctity by depicting her as a young girl free from sin, pure in mind and body, and glorified.

Artists have always portrayed the Christ Child sitting or standing on His mother's lap, with a physical posture and articulation of the body not associated with infancy, but with maturity and adult life. An infant is physically unable to sit in an upright position by itself, hold its head erect, and perform an act of benediction or blessing. Almost every Christ Child is shown in this guise. Children move from their major joints (shoulders and hips) and are, consequently, awkward and ungainly in their body movements. Donatello, the famous sculptor of fifteenth century Florence, depicted this beautifully in his dancing children and angels in the outdoor *Pulpit* (1433-1438) of the Cathedral of Prato, and in the *Cantoria* (1433-1439), the Museo dell' Opera del Duomo, Florence, originally in the Cathedral of Florence.[101] Donatello had an excellent understanding of the psychology and behavior of children and their physical limitations. By giving the Christ Child the attributes of an adult, the artist was able to distinguish between the divine and mortal child.

Michelangelo exercised the same prerogative when he represented the Madonna of the *Pietà* (who was about forty-seven years old when Christ died) as a young woman untouched by the intervening years and without any change in her physical appearance. This is demonstrated descriptively by comparing Mary (*pl. 28*) in the *Pietà* with Mary (*pl. 29*) in Michelangelo's *Bruges Madonna* (50.4"), which derives from the *Pietà* and was carved between 1501 and 1504.

Theologians believe that Mary was about fourteen years old when she was married to Joseph. This belief is based on common knowledge of Jewish marriage customs as they existed during the time of Christ. Judging from the age at which Hebrew maidens became marriageable, it is plausible that Mary gave birth to her Son when she was about thirteen or fourteen years old. No historical record exists to establish the actual age of Mary when she gave birth.[102]

Pediatricians agree that the Christ Child in the *Bruges Madonna* is about two years old. Most standard books on pediatrics reproduce a chart illustrating the physical development and the physiometric measurements of infants at various age levels. In a two-year-old child, for example, the navel is located in the center of the body. At no other age is this true, and Michelangelo must have been aware of this natural phenomenon.[103] Allowing for the slightly foreshortened position of the head in the Christ Child (*pl. 27, 31*), the navel is in the center of the body. This, together with other physical characteristics, helps to establish the fact that the Christ Child is two years old. Mary would then be about sixteen years of age. Michelangelo's desire for unity induced him to place the Christ Child between the Madonna's knees, making the two figures part of the same volume in an unusual composition.

A comparison between the two Madonnas shows that they are about the same age—sixteen years old (*pl. 28, 29*). Mary in the *Pietà* is the same youthful idealization at forty-seven as she was at sixteen. The thirty-one years that have passed between the depiction of the Christ Child and His death have not left the slightest trace of age or other physical mark on the sensitive features of the Madonna. This was Michelangelo's way of expressing her saintliness.

There are three elements in the *Pietà* that typify the High Renaissance in Italy, the period between 1500 and 1520. One is the mathematical basis of this monumental composition. The second is the self-containment, dignity and restraint shown in the sculptor's portrayal of grief and sorrow—qualities commonly found throughout the High Renaissance. And third, the integration of *form and content* is the per-

fection that every artist strove to achieve during this period and which
Michelangelo attained with notable success.

Michelangelo was only twenty-five years old when he completed
his epic monument, and his great fame and reputation spread throughout Italy and Europe.[104]

French Cardinal Jean de Bilhères de Lagraulas had asked Pope
Alexander VI (1492-1503) for permission to place a statue of the *Pietà*
in the chapel of the Kings of France—called the chapel or church of
St. Petronilla—in old St. Peter's Basilica, as a remembrance of his service
to France and the Holy See.

Michelangelo's *Pietà* was first erected in this chapel, situated in the
south transept of the church. When the church of St. Petronilla was
demolished to clear the way for the new building designed by Donato
Bramante (1444-1514), the statue was installed in the Cappella della
Vergine Maria della Febbre in 1517. This chapel was on the south side
of old St. Peter's and the statue was seen in this location by Vasari and
Condivi.[105] Bramante died soon after the new building was begun. In
1546, when Michelangelo was seventy-one years old, Pope Paul III
(1534-1549) placed him in charge of the new St. Peter's Basilica. The
present building owes most of its outstanding features to his genius.

Sometime during the pontificate of Pope Gregory XIII (1572-1585),
the *Pietà* was transferred to the Choir of Sixtus IV (1471-1484), the
fourth chapel on the south side of the church. In 1749, Pope Benedict
XIV (1740-1758) had it placed in the present chapel, called La Cappella
della Febbre (*pl. 6*), the first chapel on the north side of the new St.
Peter's. The chapel is now called La Cappella della Pietà.

In 1637 Count Alessandro Sforza di Piacenza gave St. Peter's two
bronze baroque angels holding a crown which were placed, floating in
air, above the head of the Madonna (*pl. 33*). The effect was monstrous.
In 1927, at the suggestion of Charles de Tolnay, the most distinguished
scholar on Michelangelo in modern times, the angels with their crown
were removed, together with the bronze halo on Christ's head. These
redundant accessories had marred the beauty of the *Pietà*.

The beautiful statue of the *Pietà*, a reaffirmation of the immortality
of the human soul, was Michelangelo's tribute to the Glory of God and
his contribution to the aesthetic enjoyment of man. What a fitting
testimonial to the genius of Michelangelo that his famous *Pietà* is the
highlight of the New York World's Fair of 1964, on the 400th anniversary of his death—February 18, 1564.

· P∂RT THREE ·

Pope John XXIII consents to exhibit Pietà *at World's Fair / Impact
of* Pietà *on American taste and culture / Removal of* Pietà
*from St. Peter's protested / Edward Kinney's role in
transportation of* Pietà / *Cardinal Spellman and the Elgin
transportation of* Pietà / *Cardinal Spellman and the Elgin
Marbles / Precautions taken to transport* Pietà *safely /
Official unveiling of* Pietà *in New York, April 19, 1964.*

A FRENCH CARDINAL (His Eminence Jean de Bilhères de Lagraulas)
commissioned Michelangelo in Rome to carve his celebrated *Pietà*
on August 27, 1498.[106] On March 28, 1962, an American Cardinal (His
Eminence Francis Cardinal Spellman, Archbishop of New York) made
it possible for millions of Americans to see this famous statue at the
Vatican Pavilion of the Holy See at the New York World's Fair in New
York, which opened officially on April 22, 1964.[107]

On the morning of March 28, 1962, Pope John XXIII received
Cardinal Spellman.[108] His Holiness gave the New York Archbishop his
consent to bring the *Pietà* to New York, where it was unveiled on April
19, 1964, several days before the opening of the Fair.

The historic announcement in Rome that the *Pietà* would be sent
to the New York World's Fair precipitated a chain-reaction of criticism
and protests throughout the Western world, particularly in Italy.[109] Fear
was expressed that this priceless treasure might be damaged or lost in
transit, that the risks of transportation were too great, that it could never
be replaced if a misfortune befell it, and so on.

On his return to the United States on April 3, 1962, Cardinal Spellman, who had attended a meeting of the Central Preparatory Commission for the Ecumenical Council in Rome, assured reporters that the
Pietà would be brought to this country from St. Peter's Basilica. Several
days later protests began to appear in American newspapers. Germain
Seligman, a member of the Art Committee for the New York World's Fair
of 1939, expressed strong opposition to the transportation of the *Pietà*

49

to New York, but tempered his criticism in a concluding paragraph by saying: "I want to add that we should all feel flattered and highly honored at the gesture of His Holiness so spontaneously made" because it shows that Pope John realizes the importance of the World's Fair.[110]

On the other hand, John J. McCloy, former Assistant Secretary of War in World War II, wrote to Cardinal Spellman "in appreciation of the part he played in connection with the gracious and imaginative action of His Holiness," in permitting the *Pietà* to be exhibited in New York.

The chairman of the Department of Art of the University of Pennsylvania and the Director of the Fogg Museum at Harvard University vehemently protested the transfer of the *Pietà*. The most vitriolic protests came from Europe. In Italy a group of artists demonstrated in front of the Cathedral of Florence soliciting signatures on protest petitions. A plaster cast of the *Pietà* was driven on a truck through the principal streets. Many thought that the artists had clandestinely taken the *Pietà* from St. Peter's Basilica, until it became apparent that it was a plaster replica and not the original marble.[111]

Professor Giulio Carlo Argan, professor of the history of art at the University of Rome, alarmed at the decision to transport the *Pietà* to New York, said that the project was "the most absurd that can be imagined." Similar views were expressed by art critics, art historians and artists. *Il Messaggero di Roma,* a widely read Italian newspaper, commented: "Who would like to see the *Pietà* displayed with their [the Americans'] most advanced industrial products?" It added, "tied up with ropes in a crate like a common parcel of dried fish."[112] This statement is a reference to the manner in which the heavily crated *Pietà* had been hoisted aboard the S.S. *Cristoforo Colombo,* the Italian ship that carried the statue to the United States.

What troubled the Italians was the fact that the year 1964 is the 400th anniversary of the death of Michelangelo. The *Pietà*, which had been carved in Rome, had never left the Eternal City since the Florentine sculptor had completed it in 1499 or 1500 (the exact date is not known) and the Italians were piqued at the thought that it should be removed from Rome on the anniversary of the artist's death.

Professor Karl Hatlaub of Heidelberg is reported as saying: "There must be a mistake." Munich and Vienna critics were particularly caustic in their criticism. And so were the English critics. However, in spite of the opposition, Pope John XXIII remained firm.

To assuage the fears of those concerned with the risks involved in transporting the *Pietà* to the United States, it should be recalled that in

1506, Michelangelo's *Bruges Madonna* was shipped safely from Florence to northwest Belgium.[113] Notwithstanding the primitive means of transportation in the sixteenth century, the *Bruges Madonna* was delivered to the Church of Notre-Dame in Bruges without mishap. Modern transportation facilities and the scientific knowledge of packing and crating made a tragic misadventure unlikely. To this assurance was added the fact that museums and private collections throughout the United States are filled with thousands of European and Asian art treasures and that the great majority were taken to these shores without loss or damage. True, there are always risks. But the thorough and painstaking planning of the McNally Brothers, New York packers and shippers, and the Daniel F. Young Corporation, shipping experts, working in collaboration with the Vatican's chief engineer, Dr. Francesco Vacchini, was a guarantee that the *Pietà* would be brought to the United States with extreme prudence and with every precaution humanly possible. Edward M. Kinney, director of purchasing and shipping for the New York Office of Catholic Relief Services, an affiliate of the National Catholic Welfare Conference, had complete responsibility of overseeing the entire operation and of the elaborate and scientific planning to safeguard the *Pietà* from any possible damage.

Impelled by the desire to give all Americans the joy and exhilaration of seeing Christianity's greatest statue, Cardinal Spellman, with discriminating foresight, assessed the tremendous impact the *Pietà* would have on American taste, art and culture. For the Christian world it is also an eloquent documentation of Christian faith. It was for these reasons that Cardinal Spellman had asked His Holiness, Pope John XXIII, for permission to exhibit the *Pietà* at the World's Fair in New York.

In his request Cardinal Spellman was mindful of the far-reaching influence the *Laocoön* (c. 160-130 B.C.) had on European taste and art after its discovery.[114] A sculptural group of the Greek Hellenistic period, the *Laocoön* was unearthed in Rome in 1506 during the pontificate of Pope Julius II and is now in the Vatican Museum. Artists, scholars and travelers from all parts of Europe went to Rome to see this famous Greek masterpiece. Cardinal Spellman foresees a similar influence exerted by the *Pietà* in this country.

When the announcement was made in March 1962, of the *Pietà's* pending visit to the United States, *The Tablet*, a Catholic newspaper published in London, printed an article critical of the forthcoming event.[115] Several months after this article appeared, Cardinal Spellman entertained a house guest from England, His Grace, the Most Reverend

John Carmel Heenan, Archbishop of Liverpool (now John Cardinal Heenan, Archbishop of Westminster and Primate of England).

On June 4, 1962, Cardinal Spellman presided at the commencement of the College of New Rochelle, a Catholic college for women in the Archdiocese of New York. Archbishop Heenan attended the ceremonies as a candidate for an honorary degree.[116] During the graduation exercises, Cardinal Spellman, with characteristic good humor, referred to the criticism of the London *Tablet* and to the detractions made by critics regarding the *Pietà*. He remarked that he did not understand why so many people were concerned about the *Pietà* as he had every intention of returning it to St. Peter's Basilica in Rome at the close of the World's Fair. He then added in jest that the *Pietà* would not suffer the same fate as the Elgin Marbles. Archbishop Heenan, together with the graduating seniors and their guests, chuckled at the reference. Apparently the pun was directed at the unduly captious and vituperative critics, regarding the removal of the *Pietà* from Rome.

Mention of the Elgin Marbles was a reference to the sculptures removed from the famous Greek Parthenon (447-438 B.C.) in Athens, by Thomas Bruce (1766-1841), the seventh Earl of Elgin, between 1803 and 1812.[117] Lord Elgin had served as British envoy extraordinary to Constantinople from 1799 to 1802. He was denounced by many Englishmen for removing the priceless sculptures from Greece's most renowned building and transporting them to England. Lord Byron called him a "dishonest and rapacious vandal," but modern England has made him a national hero. At the time the Greek marbles were taken, Greece was governed by the Turks. Lord Elgin claimed to have obtained permission from the Turks before shipping the ancient treasures to England.

In 1810, Lord Elgin published a *Memorandum* defending his actions. The British Parliament not only exonerated him, but also purchased the sculptures from him for £35,000. These sculptures, referred to as the Elgin Marbles, represent the most prized possession of the British Museum.

In modern times the Greek government has made repeated requests to the British for the return of the Elgin Marbles to enable it to restore the Parthenon to its original splendor. The British have remained unresponsive.

The 6,700-pound *Pietà*, insured for six million dollars, left Naples on April 5, 1964 on board the *Cristoforo Colombo* and arrived in New York on April 13, 1964 without incident. When it left Naples, it was hoisted by a crane and lowered carefully on the sundeck of the ship, where it was fixed to the deck with hydrostatic fasteners designed to open automatically in case of shipwreck or other disaster. Gripping hooks were built into the outer steel case to prevent it from moving, shifting or vibrating. The outer steel case, manufactured in the United States, was completely airtight, watertight and was designed to float in water. It was painted white with bright red corners to facilitate identification if it had been catapulted into the sea. If the ship had gone down, special transmitters attached to the outer case would have flashed light beacons visible fifteen miles at sea level and fifty miles by air, and radio directional signals would have been broadcast, to assist those trying to locate the six-ton crate—the combined weight of the statue and the three containers.

Before the *Pietà* was packed, X-rays and Cobalt-6o gamma-ray photographs were taken to determine if the marble statue had invisible flaws. None was found.

Before lowering the statue on its vibration-proof platform, the fingers of the Madonna's left hand, which had been broken and restored in the eighteenth century, were carefully wrapped in gauze and secured with heavy surgical adhesive. Heavy lumber was then used to build an enclosure around the open platform to form the first case. It was lined with thick layers of polystyrene and packed tight with thousands of polystyrene beads, which filled all the recesses, cavities and spaces of the statue to give it full protection against shock and dislocation. This plastic had sufficient buoyancy to keep the six-ton weight afloat.

The first case was then placed in a second wooden case and the space between the two cases was again packed tightly with shock-absorbing polystyrene. By this method of packing, the first case was actually suspended in the second one. The second crate was then slipped into the steel container and set on an eight-inch layer of polystyrene, separated with plywood to obtain equal distribution of the weight. A heavy asbestos lining was used in the steel case for fireproofing and the space between the wooden case and steel container was also filled with polystyrene. It was then hermetically sealed. The statue was actually packed in three cases fitting inside each other.[118]

On its arrival in New York, the valuable crate was lifted from the sundeck of the *Cristoforo Colombo* and lowered on *The Challenger,* the barge that transported it around the Battery at the southern end of Manhattan and up the East River into Flushing Bay, where it was loaded on a flatbed trailer and brought to the Vatican Pavilion of the New York World's Fair in Flushing.

On Sunday, April 19, 1964, before an assembly of distinguished church and government dignitaries, the famous *Pietà* was unveiled. It is exhibited dramatically on a rather high pedestal raised on two steps. A large Cross with a shroud hanging from its horizontal bar is set against the wall behind the statue.

Michelangelo left a very thin marble base for his *Pietà*, preferring to utilize the full dimensions of the original block of marble for his two figures. A thin base, however, is not a suitable foundation for large figures. For this reason, the statue itself was set on a thick platform. It was shown in this manner in St. Peter's Basilica, except that in the Vatican Pavilion the *Pietà* is properly positioned.

A strong light from the upper right-hand corner of the exhibition area is focused directly on the *Pietà*. The light reflected from Christ's reclining body illuminates the Madonna's face. Flickering lights in blue glass receptacles, simulating votive candles, are arranged vertically from floor to ceiling and are secured by wires. Several rows of these small lights, set at different levels, flank each side of the statue in the foreground. The psychological effect of the interior design heightens the religious and aesthetic impact of the statue itself. Bulletproof glass is used as a protective screen across the entire front of the exhibition area.

Visitors desiring to see the *Pietà* have a choice of four vantage stations. There are three mechanical platforms, set at different heights, which give the spectator an unobstructed view while he is carried across the width of the exhibition area. The lowest one carries the spectator across the whole area at eye level. The other two automated platforms show the statue slightly below eye level. The fourth viewing platform is stationary and is intended for those who desire to linger longer to contemplate the *Pietà's* great beauty. This platform is the furthest one back and the highest of all the viewing walks.

The drama and poignancy of the story told so beautifully by Michelangelo in this sacred theme is a reminder that in the death of Christ, Christianity was born and with it a new creed and a new way of life for all mankind.

"And He answering said, thou shalt love the Lord thy God
with all thy heart, and with all thy soul, and with
all thy strength, and with all thy mind;
and thy neighbor as thyself."

NOTES

1 Clark, Kenneth, *The Nude: A Study in Ideal Form*, 241-242. Redig de Campos, "Un nuovo aspetto della Pietà di Michelangelo in San Pietro," 100-101.

2 Ricciotti, *The Life of Christ*, 631. *Golgotha* is Aramaic, *Calvaria* is Latin, *Gulgoleth* is Hebrew.

3 Tolnay, *The Youth of Michelangelo*, Vol. I, 145. Height 174 cm; greatest width, 195 cm; greatest depth, 64 cm. Redig de Campos, *op. cit.*, 101, in a recent measurement the Pietà measured 172 cm.

4 Condivi, *Vita di Michelangelo*, 2-3, 89. Michelangelo's mother, Francesca, was the daughter of Neri di Miniato del Sera and Maria Bonda Rucellai. Vasari (Gaetano Milanesi, ed.), *Le opere di Giorgio Vasari*, Vol. VII, 136. Papini, *Vita di Michelangiolo nella vita del suo tempo*, 12-13. Holroyd, *Michael Angelo Buonarroti*, 6. Tolnay, *op. cit.*, 11.

5 Vasari, *op. cit.*, 136-137. Papini, *op. cit.*, 13. Condivi, *op. cit.*, 3.

6 Tolnay, *op. cit.*, 11. Vasari, *op. cit.*, 137.

7 Vasari, *ibid.* Papini, *op. cit.*, 17-19.

8 Symonds, *The Life of Michelangelo*, 6. Vasari, *op. cit.*, 137-138. Papini, *op. cit.*, 24. Condivi, *op. cit.*, 3.

9 Tolnay, *op. cit.*, 14. Vasari, *op. cit.*, 138.

10 Vasari, *ibid.* Vasari states that Michelangelo was fourteen years old when he entered Domenico Ghirlandaio's studio, but he was in error.

11 Condivi, *op. cit.*, 5.

12 Pope-Hennessy, *Italian Renaissance Sculpture*, 101, 319. Vasari, *op. cit.*, 141-142. Tolnay, *op. cit.*, 16. Symonds, *op. cit.*, 13.

13 Condivi, *op. cit.*, 5-6. Vasari, *op. cit.*, 142-143.

14 Vasari, *ibid.* Condivi, *op. cit.*, 7.

15 Vasari, *op. cit.*, 143. Vasari (1568, Fiorenza), 721. Tolnay, *op. cit.*, 17.

16 Tolnay, *ibid.* Vasari, *op. cit.*, 143.

17 Robb, *Neoplatonism of the Italian Renaissance*, 58, 62, 90. Tolnay, *op. cit.*, 18. Condivi, *op. cit.*, 8. Holroyd, *op. cit.*, 13-14.

18 Vasari (1568), 27. Condivi, *op. cit.*, 26ff.

19 Maffei, *Michelangelo's Lost St. John*, 15.

20 Vasari (1568), 252. "Se la vita ci piace, essendo anco la morte di mano d'un medesimo maestro, quella non ci dovrebbe dispiacere."

21 Symonds, *op. cit.*, 25-27. Condivi, *op. cit.*, 8-9. Vasari, *op. cit.*, 145.

22 Symonds, *op. cit.*, 29-30. Holroyd, *op. cit.*, 16-17. Condivi, *op. cit.*, 9-10.

23 Poggi, "Della prima partenza di Michelangelo Buonarroti da Firenze," 33ff. Vasari, *op. cit.*, 146. Condivi, *op. cit.*, 10. Tolnay, *op. cit.*, 20-22.

24 Vasari, *op. cit.*, 146. Holroyd, *op. cit.*, 19.

25 Schevill, *History of Florence from the Founding of the City through the Renaissance*, 437-438, 443, 470. Condivi, *op. cit.*, 11.

26 Young, *The Medici*, 227-228.

27 Holroyd, *op. cit.*, 19. Condivi, *op. cit.*, 11.

28 Schevill, *op. cit.*, 437.

29 Vasari, *op. cit.*, 146-147. Vasari (1568), 35. Condivi, *op. cit.*, 10-11. Tolnay, *op. cit.*, 22.

30 Vasari, *op. cit.*, 146. Condivi, *op. cit.*, 11. Tolnay, *op. cit.*, 137, 139, 141.

31 Condivi, *op. cit.*, 12. Vasari (1568), 147.

32 Condivi, *op. cit.*, 12.

33 Maffei, *op. cit.*, 35, 37. Guasti, *Di Cafaggiolo e d'altre fabbriche di ceramiche in Toscana*, 73.

34 Maffei, *op. cit.*, 8.

35 *Ibid.*, Plate 28.

36 *Ibid.*, 15. Clark, *op. cit.*, 247. Condivi, *op. cit.*, 7. Vasari, *op. cit.*, 145.
37 Maffei, *op. cit.*, Plates 28, 30, 32, 34, 36, 38.
38 *Ibid.*, *passim.* Vasari, *op. cit.*, 175. Crowe & Cavalcaselle, *A New History of Painting in Italy*, III, 445, 448.
39 Berenson, *Aesthetics and History*, 24, 28-29. Panofsky, *Meaning in the Visual Arts*, 36ff.
40 Letter to Piero Tozzi, April 10, 1956.
41 Vasari, *op. cit.*, 147. Holroyd, *op. cit.*, 23.
42 Tolnay, *op. cit.*, 26, 55.
43 Symonds, *op. cit.*, 35.
44 Vasari, *op. cit.*, 150-151. Condivi, *op. cit.*, 13-14. Holroyd, *op. cit.*, 24-25, 107-108. Tolnay, *op. cit.*, 27, 142, 203. Symonds, *op. cit.*, 37-42.
45 Schevill, *op. cit.*, 508. He "remained throughout his life a true Christian believer and an earnest communicant of the Catholic church."
46 Morgan, *The Life of Michelangelo*, 12.
47 Robb, *op. cit.*, 225-227.
48 Morgan, *op. cit.*, 12.
49 Vasari, *op. cit.*, 163. Tolnay, *op. cit.*, 27, 146. Redig de Campos, *op. cit.*, 98. This Vatican scholar has definitely established that the French Cardinal's name was Jean de Bilhères de Lagraulas, and not Jean de Villiers de la Groslaye, as many writers record. In a letter to the author, dated January 24, 1964. Dr. Redig de Campos writes: "Sul cardinale Jean de Bilhères de Lagraulas, queste è il nome corretto." Even Tolnay repeats this error (146). Redig de Campos, *Raffaello e Michelangelo*, 103.
50 Milanesi (ed.), *Le Lettere di Michelangelo Buonarroti*, 163-164.

> *Roma, 27 d'agosto 1498*
> *Allogazione a Michelangelo*
> *del gruppo di marmo della*
> *Pietà in Roma.*
>
> *Die XXVII mensis augusti 1498*
> *Sia nota et manifesto a che legerà la presente scripta, come el reverendissimo cardinal di San Dionisio si è convenuto con maestro Michelangelo statuario fiorentino, che lo dicto maestro debia far una Pietà di marmo a sue spese, ciò è una Vergene Maria vestita, con Cristo morto in braccio, grande quanto sia vno*

> *homo insto, per prezo di ducati quattrocento cinquanta d'oro in oro papali, in termino di uno anno dal di della principiata opera. Et lo dicto reverendissimo Cardinale promette farli lo pagamento in questo modo, ciò è: Imprimis promette darli ducati centocinquanta d'oro in oro papali, innanti che comenzi l'opera: et da poi principiata l'opera promette ogni quattro mesi darli ducati cento simili al dicto Michelangelo, in modo che il dicti quatro cento cinquanta ducati d'oro in oro papali siano finiti di pagarli in vno anno, se la dicta opera sarà finita; et se prima sarà finita, che la sua reverendissima Signoria prima sia obligata a pagarlo del tutto.*
> *Et io Iacobo Gallo prometto al reverendissimo Monsignore che lo dicto Michelangelo farà la dicta opera in fra uno anno et sarà la più bella opera di marmo che sia hoge in Roma, et che maestro nisuno la faria megliore hoge. Et si versa vice prometto al ditto Michelangelo che lo reverendissimo Cardinale la farà lo pagamento secundo che de sopra è scripto. Et a fede io Iacobo Gallo ho facta la presente di mia propria mano, anno, mese et di sopradito. Intendendosi per questa scripta esser cassa et annullata ogni altra scripta di mano mia, o vero di mano del dicto Michelangelo, et questa solo habia effecto.*
> *Hane dati il dicto reverendissimo Cardinale a me Iacobo più tempo fa ducati cento d'oro in oro di Camera et a di dicto ducati cinquanta d'oro in oro papali.*
> *Ita est Ioannes, Cardinalis S. Dyonisij.*
> *Idem Iacobus Gallus manu propria.*

51 Milanesi, *op. cit.*, 163.
52 Janson, *History of Art*, 259. Panofsky, *Meaning in the Visual Arts*, 37.
53 Janson, *op. cit.*, 259-260.
54 Janson, *op. cit.*, 259, Fig. 408.
55 Morey, *Medieval Art*, 355.
56 Morey, *op. cit.*, 350.
57 Morey, *op. cit.*, 384-385.
58 Clements, *Michelangelo's Theory of Art*, 161.
59 Panofsky, *Studies in Iconology*, 171.
60 Berenson, *Italian Pictures of the Renaissance*, Vol. II, Plate 998.

61 Clements, *op. cit.*, 159.
62 Berenson, *op. cit.*, Vol. I, 196; Vol. II, Plate 1100.
63 Pope-Hennessy, *Italian High Renaissance and Baroque Sculpture*, Cat. Vol., 6.
64 Supino, *L'Arte nelle Chiese di Bologna*, 81.
65 Tolnay, *op. cit.*, 92.
66 Clements, *op. cit.*, 160.
67 Schubring, *Luca della Robbia und seine Familie*, 72, Plates 70, 71.
68 Tolnay, *op. cit.*, 91.
69 Planiscig, *Luca della Robbia*, 36.
70 Janson, *The Sculpture of Donatello*, 14-16.
71 Blunt, *Artistic Theory in Italy*, 59, 61-62, 69, Clements, *op. cit.*, 10.
72 Panofsky, *Meaning in the Visual Arts*, 36ff. Berenson, *Aesthetics and History*, 28-29.
73 Vasari, *op. cit.*, 151. Condivi, *op. cit.*, 14. "Col Figliuol morto in grembo."
74 Antonio Rottino, M.D., Ph.D., Director of Pathology, St. Vincent's Hospital, New York County, and Professor of Pathology at New York University School of Medicine and Post-Graduate Medical School. Milton Helpern, M.D., Chief Medical Examiner, City of New York, world-renowned pathologist. Louis L. Bergmann, M.D., Professor of Anatomy, New York University School of Medicine and Post-Graduate Medical School.
75 Vasari, *op. cit.*, 146. "Fece per la Chiesa di Santo Spirito della città di Firenze un Crocifisso di legno." Condivi, *op. cit.*, 9. The Church of Santo Spirito in Florence consists of a church, a monastery and a hospital with a mortuary. Holroyd, *op. cit.*, 16. *Life Magazine*, Vol. 56, No. 8, February 21, 1964, 45-46, 49-52. Dr. Margrit Lisner, a German art historian, rediscovered Michelangelo's painted wooden Crucifix, which he had carved in 1493 when he was eighteen years old. It hung above the high altar in the Church of Santo Spirito until about 1600, when it was removed during alterations of the church and lost. The Crucifix is smaller than life-size and painted according to the practice of the time. It is 4' 5" high.
76 Blunt, *op. cit.*, 61. Tolnay, *op. cit.*, 20, 52. Symonds, *op. cit.*, 28.

77 Redig de Campos, "Un nuovo aspetto della Pietà di Michelangelo," 100-101.
78 Tolnay, *op. cit.*, Fig. 32.
79 Korte, *"Deutsche Vesperbilder in Italien,"* 1ff. Clements, *op. cit.*, 33. Tolnay, *op. cit.*, 148. Pope-Hennessy, *Italian High Renaissance and Baroque Sculpture*, 6.
80 Tolnay, *op. cit.*, 149.
81 With the permission of Francis Cardinal Spellman, Archbishop of New York, the author measured the figure of Christ at the Vatican Pavilion, October 14, 1964. Overall dimensions of figure, 74" or six feet and two inches. Length of head from hairline to end of beard, 10". From the hairline of the head to the notch of the neck, 12". From the notch of the neck to the navel, 14". From hip to knee, 23". From knee to bottom of foot, 23". Width of shoulders, 19". Left calf, 15¼". Left ankle, 9½". Right calf, 15". Right ankle, 9⅝". Length of left foot from heel to large toe, 9¾". Length of right foot, 10½".
82 Pope-Hennessy, *Italian High Renaissance and Baroque Sculpture*, Plate Vol., Plate 6. 174 cm. Tolnay, *op. cit.*, 145. Kriegbaum, *Michelangelo Buonarroti, Die Bildwerke*, 42, 175 cm. Redig de Campos, "Un nuovo aspetto della Pietà di Michelangelo in San Pietro," 101, 172 cm.
83 Tolnay, *The Medici Chapel*, 55, 139, 178 cm.; 141-144, 173 cm. Pope-Hennessy, *Italian High Renaissance and Baroque Sculpture*, Plate Vol., Plate 24. 173 cm.
84 Clements, *op. cit.*, 33.
85 Gaye, *Carteggio inedito d'artisti dei secoli XIV. XV. XVI*, 500. Tolnay, *op. cit.*, 92.
86 Vasari, *op. cit.*, 152. Redig de Campos, *Raffaello e Michelangelo*, 110.
87 Pittaluga, *Filippo Lippi*, 135, Plate 13.
88 Tolnay, *op. cit.*, 92.
89 Mackowsky, *Verrocchio*, 50-51. Pope-Hennessy, *Italian Renaissance Sculpture*, 40, 312-313, Fig. 57, Plates 80, 81.
90 Venturi, *Michelangelo*, 40.
91 Planiscig, *Donatello*, Plates 173, 175.
92 Tolnay, *op. cit.*, 145.
93 Condivi (Anton Francesco Gori, ed.), *op. cit.*, 14.

*"Non sai tu che le donne caste,
moltopiù fresche si mantengono, che
le non caste? Quanto maggioremente
una Vergine, nella qualle non cadde
mai pur un minimo lascivo desiderio, che alterasse quel corpo? Anzi
ti vo' dir di più, che tal freschezza e
fior di gioventù, altrocchè per tal
natural via in lei si mantenne, è
anco credibile che per divin' opera
fosse aiutato a comprovare al mondo
le verginità e purità della Madonna.
Il che non fu necessario nel Figliuolo: anzi piuttosto il contrario; per-
ciocchè volendo mostrare, che 'l
Figliuol di Dio prendesse, come
presso, veramente corpo umano, e
sottoposto a tutto quelchè un ordi-
nario uomo soggiace, eccettochè al
peccato; non bisognò col divino tener
indierto l'umano, ma lasciarlo nel
corso, ed ordine suo, sicchè quel
tempo mostrasse, che aveva ap-
punto. Pertanto non t' hai da mara-
vigliare, se per tal rispetto io feci la
Santissima Vergine, Madre d'Iddio,
a comparazion del Figliuolo assai
più giovane di quelchè quell' età or-
dinariamente ricerca, e 'l Figliuolo
lasciai nell' età Sua."*

94 Robb, *op. cit.*, 227.
95 Robb, *op. cit.*, 225, 227-228.
96 Robb, *op. cit.*, 59, 62, 225.
97 Robb, *op. cit.*, 62, 241.
98 Schevill, *op. cit.*, 440-441, 444-445,
454. Redig de Campos, *Raffaello e
Michelangelo*, 102.
99 Schevill, *op. cit.*, 416.
100 Panofsky, *Meaning in the Visual
Arts*, 158, and *Studies in Iconology*,
180. Clark, *op. cit.*, 59. Vermeule,
*European Art and the Classical
Past*, 72.
101 Janson, *Donatello*, 108ff, Plates
47a to 47c, 48a to 48g; 199ff, Plates
49a to 49c, 50.
102 Ricciotti, *op. cit.*, 231. *The Catholic
Encyclopedia*, Vol. xv, 464H. Letter to the author, January 21, 1964,
from the Rev. Earl J. Weiss, S.J.,
Dogmatic Theology Editor, *The
New Catholic Encyclopedia*, Catholic University of America, Washington, D.C.

103 Vincent James Fontana, M.D., Med-
ical Director, New York Foundling
Hospital; Director of Pediatrics, St.
Vincent's Hospital, New York
County; Clinical Professor of Pedi-
atrics, New York University School
of Medicine and Post-Graduate
Medical School. Wallace W. Mc-
Crory, M.D., Professor of Pediatrics,
Cornell University Medical College;
Chief Pediatrician, The New York
Hospital-Cornell Medical Center.
Henry R. Shinefield, M.D., Associate
Professor of Pediatrics, New York
Hospital-Cornell Medical Center.
Nelson, *Textbook of Pediatrics*, 15.
104 Condivi, *op. cit.*, 14-15.
105 Condivi, *Ibid.* Vasari, *op. cit.*, 151.
Redig de Campos, *Raffaello e Michelangelo*, 109-110.
106 Vasari, *op. cit.*, 163-164.
107 *New York Times*, March 3, 1962, 24.
108 *Ibid.*
109 *New York Times*, April 2, 1962, 12.
110 *New York Times*, April 4, 1962, 10.
New York Times, April 23, 1962.
111 *New York Times*, May 7, 1962, 30.
New York Times, May 25, 1962, 32.
New York Times, April 2, 1962, 12.
112 *The Tablet*, London, April 7, 1962,
328.
113 Tolnay, *op. cit.*, 156.
114 Richter, *A Handbook of Greek Art*,
163. *A Short General Guide to the
Pontifical Monuments, Museums
and Galleries*, 39-40.
115 *The Tablet*, *op. cit.*, 328.
116 College of New Rochelle, *Commencement Program*, June 4, 1962.
117 Walters, *The Art of the Greeks*, 99.
Robertson, *A Handbook of Greek
and Roman Architecture*, 113. "The
condition and apparent prospects at
the opening of the nineteenth century, when Greece was still part of
Turkey, went far to justify Lord
Elgin in removing to England much
of the friezes and almost all that
was left of the pedimental sculpture."
118 *Business Week*, McGraw-Hill, April
11, 1964, 32-33.

SELECTED BIBLIOGRAPHY

A Short General Guide to the Pontifical Monuments, Museums and Galleries, The Vatican City, 1950.

Berenson, Bernard, *Italian Pictures of the Renaissance, Florentine School*, Vols. I and II, London, 1963.

————, *Aesthetics and History*, New York, 1948.

Blunt, Anthony, *Artistic Theory in Italy, 1450-1600*, Oxford, 1956.

Catholic Encyclopedia, xv, New York, 1912.

Clark, Kenneth, *The Nude: A Study in Ideal Form*, New York: Pantheon Books, 1956.

Clements, Robert J., *Michelangelo's Theory of Art*, New York, 1961.

Condivi, Ascanio (Anton Francesco Gori, ed.), *Vita di Michelangelo Buonarroti*, Firenze, 1746, 2nd Edition.

Crowe, J. A., and Cavalcaselle, G. B., *A New History of Painting in Italy*, Vol. III, London and New York, 1909.

Gaye, Giovanni (ed.), *Carteggio inedito d'artisti dei secoli* xiv. xv. xvi., Vol. II, Firenze, 1840.

Guasti, Gaetano, *Di Cafaggiolo e d'altre fabbriche di ceramiche in Toscana*, Firenze, 1902.

Historical and Artistic Guide to the Basilica of Saint Domenic in Bologna, Provincial Tourist Board, Bologna Dominican Study, Bologna, 1950.

Holroyd, Charles, *Michael Angelo Buonarroti*, Life of the Master by his scholar, Ascanio Condivi, and Three Dialogues from the Portuguese by Francisco d'Ollanda, London & New York, 1903.

Janson, H. W., and Dora Lane Janson, *History of Art*, Englewood Cliffs (N.J.), n.d. [1962].

Janson, H. W., *The Sculpture of Donatello*, Princeton, 1963.

Korte, W., "Deutsche Vesperbilder in Italien," in *Kunstgesch. Jahrbuch der Bibliotheca Hertziana*, Vol. I, 1937.

Kriegbaum, F., *Michelangelo Buonarroti, Die Bildwerke*, Berlin, 1940.

Mackowsky, Hans, *Verrocchio*, Bielefeld und Leipzig, 1901.

Maffei, Fernanda de', *Michelangelo's Lost St. John; the Story of a Discovery*, New York, 1964.

Marquand, Allan, *Luca della Robbia*, London, 1914.

Milanesi, Gaetano (ed.), *Le Lettere di Michelangelo Buonarroti, pubblicate coi ricordi ed i contratti artistichi*, Firenze, 1875.

Morey, Charles Rufus, *Medieval Art*, New York, 1942.

Morgan, Charles H., *The Life of Michelangelo*, New York, 1960.

Nelson, Waldo E. (ed.), *Textbook of Pediatrics*, Philadelphia & London, 1954, 6th Edition.

Panofsky, Erwin, *Studies in Iconology*, New York, 1939.

————, *Meaning in the Visual Arts*, New York, 1955.

Papini, Giovanni, *Vita di Michelangiolo nella vita del suo tempo*, Milano, 1949.

Pittaluga, Mary, *Filippo Lippi*, Firenze, 1949.

Planiscig, Leo, *Luca della Robbia*, Wien, 1940.

————, *Donatello*, Firenze, 1947.

Poggi, Giovanni, "Della prima partenza di Michelangelo Buonarroti da Firenze," *Rivista d'Arte*, IV, 1906.

Pope-Hennessy, John, *Italian Renaissance Sculpture*, London, 1958.

————, *Italian High Renaissance and Baroque Sculpture*, Catologue Volume, London, 1963.

————, *Italian High Renaissance and Baroque Sculpture*, Plates Volume, London, 1963.

Redig de Campos, Deoclecio, *Raffaello e Michelangelo*, Roma, 1946.

————, "Un nuovo aspetto della Pietà di Michelangelo in San Pietro," *Fede e Arte, Rivista Internazionale di Arte Sacra*, Città del Vaticano, No. 1, Gennaio-Marzo, 1963.

Ricciotti, Rev. Giuseppe, *The Life of Christ*, Milwaukee, 1947.

Richter, M. A. Gisela, *A Handbook of Greek Art*, London, 1959.

Robb, Nesca A., *Neoplatonism of the Italian Renaissance*, London, 1935.

Robertson, D. S., *A Handbook of Greek and Roman Architecture*, Cambridge, 1954.

Schevill, Ferdinand, *History of Florence from the Founding of the City through the Renaissance*, New York, 1961.

Schubring, Paul, *Luca della Robbia und seine Familie*, Bielefeld und Leipzig, 1921.

Supino, Jacopo B., *L'Arte nelle Chiese di Bologna*, Secoli XV-XVI, Bologna, 1938.

Symonds, John Addington, *The Life of Michelangelo*, New York, n.d. [1936].

Tolnay, Charles de, *The Youth of Michelangelo*, Vol. I, Princeton, 1947.

————, *The Medici Chapel*, Vol. III, Princeton, 1948.

Vasari, Giorgio, *Vita del Gran Michelangelo Buonarroti*, Firenze, 1568.

————, (Gaetano Milanesi, ed.), *Le vite de' più eccellenti pittori, scultori ed architettori*, 1878-1885 (9 vols.), Vol. VII, Firenze, 1881.

Venturi, Adolfo, *Michelangelo*, London & New York, 1928.

Vermeule, Cornelius, *European Art and the Classical Past*, Cambridge, 1964.

Walters, H. B., *The Art of the Greeks*, London, 1934, 2d Edition.

Young, G. F., *The Medici*, New York, 1933.

INDEX

A

Aldovrandi, Gianfrancesco, 19
Alexander VI, 48
Argan, Giulio Carlo, 50
Argus Guarding Jo, 21
Asip, Rt. Rev. Msgr. James W., 10

B

Bacchus, 20, 21, 22, 25-26, 44
Baroque, 12
Benedict XIV, 48
Benivieni, Girolamo, 14
Berenson, Bernard, 24
Bergmann, Louis L., M.D., 9, N 74
Bigio, Nanni di Baccio, 41
Boccaccio, 19
Boland, Most Rev. Thomas A.,
    Archbishop of Newark, 10
Bologna, 18, 19, 20, 22
Bramante, Donato, 48
Brancacci Chapel, 13
Brizio, Francesco, 22
Bruce, Thomas, 52
Bruges Madonna, 22, 44, 47, 51
Bugiardini, Giuliano, 22
Byron, Lord, 52

C

Canossa, Counts of, 12
Cappella della Febbre, 11, 48
Caprese, 12
Cardiere, Andrea, 18, 19
Cathedral of Florence, 17
Centaurs, Battle of the, 15, 17-18, 21
Charles VIII (King of France),
    18, 19, 28
Christ, 17
Christ Child, 15, 16, 17
Cicognani, Cardinal Amleto Giovanni,
    Papal Secretary of State, 9
Clark, Kenneth, 24
Clements, Robert J., 30
Comber, Most Rev. John W., M.M., 10
Condivi, Ascanio, 9, 15, 17, 18, 19, 20,
    21, 34, 37, 44, 45, 48
Cooke, Rt. Rev. Msgr. Terence J.,
    Chancellor of the Archdiocese of
    New York, 9, 10
Correggio (Antonio Allegri), 22
Costello, Rt. Rev. Msgr. Francis M., 10
Council, Ecumenical, 11, 49
Creation of Adam, Sistine Ceiling, 40
Cushing, Richard Cardinal, Archbishop
    of Boston, 10

D

Dante, 19
DeBellis, Hannibal, M.D., 9
Desiderio (da Settignano), 15
Donatello, 13, 15, 17, 33, 43, 46;
    Apostles' Doors, 17; Cantoria, 46;
    Judith Slaying Holofernes, 43;
    Pulpit, Cathedral of Prato, 46;
    St. John the Evangelist, 33
Doni Madonna (Holy Family), 44

E

Elgin, Lord (see Thomas Bruce)
Elgin Marbles (British Museum), 52
Entombment, 30

F

Ficino, Marsilio, 14, 45
Flynn, Rt. Rev. Msgr. Timothy J., 10
Fontana, Vincent James, M.D., 9, N 103
Form and content, 47-48

G

Gallo, Jacopo, 25, 28
Ghiberti, Lorenzo, 16
Ghirlandaio, Benedetto, 13, 30
Ghirlandaio, Davide, 13
Ghirlandaio, Domenico, 13, 22
Ghirlandaio, Ridolfo, 13
Giovanni, Bertoldo di, 13
Golgotha, 12
Gorman, Rt. Rev. Msgr. John J., 10
Gothic sculpture, 29
Granacci, Francesco, 13
Greece, 52
Gregory XIII, 48

H

Heenan, John Cardinal, Archbishop of
    Westminster and Primate of
    England, 52
Helpern, Milton, M.D., 9, N 74
Hermes, 21, 39
Holy Family (Doni Madonna), 44
Humanism, 45

J

Joel, Prophet, Sistine Ceiling, 40
John XXIII, 11, 49, 50, 51
Judgment of Paris, 15
Julius II, 24
Juno, 15

K

Kellenberg, Most Rev. Walter P.,
 Bishop of Rockville Centre, 10
Kinney, Edward M., 10, 51
Krol, Most Rev. John J., Archbishop of
 Philadelphia, 10

L

LaFarge, Henry A., 9
Landino, Cristoforo, 14
Lagraulas, Cardinal Jean de Bilhères
 de, 27, 28-29, 31, 39, 48, 49, N 49
Lahey, Rev. Joseph T., 10
Laocoön, 51
Last Judgment, Sistine Ceiling, 39
Leonard, Rt. Rev. Msgr. Raymond S., 10
Leonardo da Vinci, 21, 32, 42;
 Adoration of the Magi, 32;
 Last Supper, 32, 42
Lippi, Fra Filippo, 41; Madonna
 Enthroned (Louvre), 41
Lironi, Giuseppe, 43
Lisner, Margrit, 37, N 75
Lombardo, Josef Vincent, 9, 64, N 81
Louis XI (King of France), 28
Lysippos, 39; Agias, 39

M

Madonna della Febbre, 11
Madonna of the Stairs, 15-17, 21, 40
Maffei, Fernanda de', 22
Mannerism, 12
Masaccio, 13
McCloy, John J., 50
McCrory, Wallace W., M.D., 9, N 103
McEntegart, Most Rev. Bryan J.,
 Bishop of Brooklyn, 9
McIntyre, James Francis Cardinal,
 Archbishop of Los Angeles, 10
Medici Chapel, 17, 40
Medici Collection, 15, 21, 22
Medici, Cosimo de', 14
Medici, Giuliano de' (Duke of
 Nemours), 39, 40
Medici, Lorenzo de' (The Magnificent),
 13, 14, 15, 18, 21, 40, 44
Medici, Lorenzo de' (Duke of Urbino),
 40
Medici, Lorenzo di Pierfrancesco de',
 20, 24
Medici, Piero de', 18, 19, 21
Meyer, Albert Cardinal, Archbishop
 of Chicago, 10
Michelangelo, Passim
 Angel, 19; Bacchus, 20, 21, 22, 24,
 25-26, 45; Battle of Cascina, 17, 18;
 Battle of the Centaurs, 15, 17-18, 21;
 Bruges Madonna, 22, 44, 47, 51;
 Creation of Adam, 40; Crucifix
 (wood), 37; St. Anne (Oxford), 42;
 Doni Madonna (Holy Family), 44;
 Giuliano de' Medici (Duke of
 Nemours), 39-40; Holy Family (see
 Doni Madonna); Last Judgment,
 18, 39; Lorenzo de' Medici (Duke of
 Urbino), 17, 40; Madonna of the
 Stairs, 15-17, 21, 40; Moses, 16, 40;

Pietà, Cathedral of Florence, 17, 40;
 Prophet Joel, 40; San Giovannino
 (see Youthful St. John the Baptist);
 San Petronius, 19; San Proculus, 19;
 Sistine Ceiling, 17, 22, 39, 40;
 Youthful St. John the Baptist, 19-24
Milanesi, Gaetano, 9
Miniato del Sera, Francesca Neri di, 12
Mirandola, Giovanni Pico della, 14, 45
Morey, Charles Rufus, 30
Moses, 16, 40

N

National Catholic Welfare Conference,
 51
Nativity, Church of Notre-Dame,
 Aigueperse, Auvergne, 30
Neoplatonism, 11, 14, 17, 22, 27, 41,
 45, 46
New Rochelle, College of, 52
New York World's Fair, 1964,
 48, 49, 50, 51
Noorian, Daniel Z., 20

O

O'Boyle, Most Rev. Patrick A.,
 Archbishop of Washington, D.C., 10
Or San Michele, Church of, 42-43

P

Panofsky, Erwin, 24, 30, 34, 46
Parthenon, 52
Paul III, 48
Petrarch, 19
Pietà, Cappella della, 11, 37, 48
Pietà, Cathedral of Florence, 17, 40
Pietà, Contract for, 28-29
Pietà, Villeneuve-les-Avignon, 30
Platonic Academy, 14, 15
Poliziano, Angelo, 14, 15
Praxiteles, 39; Hermes, 39

R

Redig de Campos, Deoclecio, 9, 37, N 1,
 N 49
Reni-Guido, 22
Riario, Cardinal Raffaele, 24
Ritter, Joseph Cardinal, Archbishop
 of St. Louis, 10
Robbia, Luca della, 32; Madonna
 Frescobaldi, 32-33; Madonna of the
 Rose Garden, 32-33
Roberti, Ercole de', 31; Pietà 31
Rome, 24
Rottino, Antonio, M.D., Ph.D., 9, N 74
Rovere, Cardinal Giovanni della, 24

S

St. John the Baptist, Youthful, 19-24
St. Petronius, 19
St. Proculus, 19
San Domenico, Church of, 19, 20, 31, 38
San Frediano, Church of, 30
San Giovannino (see Youthful St. John
 the Baptist)
San Lorenzo, Church of, 17, 40
San Pietro in Vincoli (Rome), 40
Sansovino, Andrea, 20

Santa Cecilia (bas-relief), 15
Santo Spirito, Church of, 37, 41
Savonarola, Fra Girolamo, 19, 45
Seligman, Germain, 49
Sellaio, Jacopo del, 30-31; Pietà, 30-31
Settignano, Desiderio da, 15
Sforza, Alessandro, 48
Sforza, Lodovico (Duke of Milan), 19
Shehan, Lawrence Cardinal,
    Archbishop of Baltimore, 10
Shinefield, Henry R., M.D., 9, N 103
Simoni, Ludovico di Lionardo
    Buonarroti, 12
Sistine Ceiling, 17, 22, 39, 40
Sistine Chapel, 17
Sixtus IV, 48
Sluter, Claus, 29
Solari, Cristoforo, 41
Somenzi, Paolo, 20
Spellman, Francis Cardinal,
    Archbishop of New York, 9, 49, 50,
    51, 52, N 81

Swanstrom, Most Rev. Edward E.,
    10, 51

T

Tablet, The (London), 52
Tolnay, Charles de, 9, 26, 31, 32, 38, 41
Tozzi, Piero, 19, 20

U

Urbino, Francesco da, 12

V

Vasari, Giorgio, 9, 13, 14, 15, 17, 19, 21,
    23, 25, 30, 34, 35, 41, 42, 48
Vacchini, Dott. Francesco, 51
Vatican Pavilion, 9, 49, 54
Venice, 18
Venturi, Adolfo, 43
Verrocchio, Andrea del, 42; Christ and
    St. Thomas, 42

BIOGRAPHICAL NOTES

Josef Vincent Lombardo was born in Greenwich Village of an old New York family. He attended and graduated from the Cooper Union School of Art and Architecture, where he received his early training as a creative artist.

He is a graduate of three universities and holds the *Bachelor of Fine Arts,* the *Bachelor of Arts,* the *Master of Arts* and the degree of *Doctor of Philosophy* from Columbia University. He also attended the University of Florence in Italy on a graduate fellowship where he won his *Doctor of Letters* degree in Italian Renaissance art. Villanova University conferred upon him the honorary degree of *Doctor of Laws* in recognition of his achievements. He has studied in Rome, Florence, Paris, and London and is the only American with two earned doctorates in fine arts.

Dr. Lombardo is the only American to attend the Royal Academy of Fine Arts in Florence, Italy, as an American Fellow. Michelangelo attended this academy in 1489 during its formative years.

The author of five other books, Dr. Lombardo is now at work on the *History of St. Patrick's Cathedral in New York,* an architectural and aesthetic critique, and *Freehand Drawing: From Realism to Abstraction.*

In 1950 the University of Florence awarded him its coveted University Medal—one of many honors and awards. This was the third time in the history of the University, founded in 1321, that an American was so honored. The other recipients were Myron C. Taylor, former president of United States Steel and President Franklin D. Roosevelt's personal representative to the Holy See; and General Mark W. Clark of the United States Army and World War II hero.

Dr. Lombardo has been on the professorial staff of Queens College of The City University of New York for twenty-five years. He is one of few Americans listed in Burke's Peerage, LTD., *The Author's & Writer's Who's Who* of Great Britain. His biography also appears in *Who's Who in America.*

PHOTO CREDITS

Giordani, Rome: 1, 2, 3, 4, 6, 7, 16, 19, 20, 21, 22, 23, 24, 28, 30
Hamilton Wright Corporation, Rome: 9, 10, 14, 25, 26, 32, 34
Thomas Feist, New York: 8, 15, 17, 18, 34, 35
John D. Schiff, New York: 11, 12, 13
C. Harrison Conroy, New York: 5
Anc. Etabl. Ern. Thill, Bruxelle: 27
Photo Brusselle: 29, 31
Istituto Italiano di Cultura, New York: 33